THE
ROYAL
FAMILY TODAY

CLB 1571
© 1986 Illustrations and text: Colour Library Books Ltd.,
    Guildford, Surrey, England.
Text filmsetting by Acesetters Ltd., Richmond, Surrey, England.
Printed and bound in Barcelona, Spain by Cronion, S.A.
All rights reserved.
ISBN 0 86283 418 X
D.L.B.: 21979 - 86

THE
ROYAL
FAMILY TODAY

Text by
Trevor Hall

COLOUR LIBRARY BOOKS

'If I am asked today,' said the Queen on her Silver Wedding anniversary, 'what I think about family life after twenty-five years of marriage, I can answer with simplicity and conviction: I am for it.'

We are always being told how important the family is in our society. Bishops praise it, government social policies are based on it, and charities seeking funds for the unloved point out how lucky most of us are to be members of a close-knit, caring family. The concept, like most, attracts its cynics, but in our heart of hearts we accept that there is nothing quite like the family when we need a point of reference, an anchor, a finger-post to cope with the confusions that sometime assail our entrenched, often servile attitudes to life, its meaning and the way it should be lived.

In that light it is hardly surprising that it is to a family – the Royal Family – that we should look in the wider context of our national identity, honour, pride – call it what you will. At the same time it seems quaintly eccentric, even pernicious to some, that a collection of individuals, born to their position by nothing more deserving than the whim of fortune, and said repeatedly in their defence to be as human as the rest of us, should be identified with power and influence in high places and enjoy privileges that would be the envy of millions.

It's a conundrum you can mull over for ever without really resolving. We know the hereditary principle is illogical in what we choose to label an egalitarian age. When things are going badly we resent the benefit that system confers on the Royal Family; we begrudge them their prerogatives, wince at the bowing and scraping, and deplore the expenditure of huge amounts of time and money desperately needed elsewhere. Yet, come a royal celebration or national rejoicing, we allow ourselves the luxury of absorbing the idea of a family up there presiding over our national affairs as not such a bad one after all. And there's nothing quite like the twinkle of tiaras, the jingle of the ceremonial horses' tack, the bray of trumpets and the sonorous boom of cannon in a distant park to convince us. It still doesn't make sense. It may be sheer, unthinking escapism. But it's there.

Like her grandfather King George V, and her great-great grandmother Queen Victoria, the Queen has a marked taste and affection for anniversaries and the memories they evoke. It is evident in countless of her speeches. Often, these memories involve other members of her family – if for no other reason than that many of her duties are elements of an annual royal round of which the family past and present has always been part, from the Braemar Games in Scotland, for instance, to Trooping the Colour and the Festival of Remembrance. For a century and a quarter it has been dispersed to all parts of the world for hundreds of royal visits. There are few places left for the Queen to go and not discover that one or other Royal Highness has beaten her to it.

The Queen may thus be forgiven if, in the year of her sixtieth birthday, she indulges not only in a few family memories, but also in the satisfying thought that both she and her royal relatives have done well to preserve and strengthen their position as the family unit to which we still cannot avoid turning, despite the passing of a generation of years that have been uncertain of direction, tumultuous in events, and sometimes depressing in outlook. If you have ever marvelled at how well the Royal Family – and the institution of monarchy which it serves – has come out of successive controversies and the difficulties which faced it as public attitudes towards it began to change, hindsight will already have shown that it was the concept of the family – rather than of a single monarchical figure, or of a faceless Constitution – that enabled that change in attitude to be encountered and absorbed.

When the Queen came to the throne in 1952, her family image may have seemed less significant, possibly because it was taken more for granted. Looking back, the Royal Family of post-War Britain seems a staid and over-respectable assortment of individuals, ultra-conservative in outlook, appearance, opinions and behaviour. The austerity from which the country was then only just emerging, and the profusion of monochrome newspaper, magazine and television photography in that twilight era of popular illustration in black-and-white only, lends an illusion of colourlessness to the image when compared with the dazzling effect of the high-quality colour reproduction available today.

Accordingly, the Queen's first achievement was a relatively effortless one – simply that of being a young, vivacious sovereign, set upon the throne in what were then seen as appallingly unexpected circumstances – the premature death of her father, George VI – which compounded the accident of history fifteen years earlier, when her uncle Edward VIII had abdicated 'for the woman I love'.

'Glamour' was hardly a respectable term in those days – too easily linked with the brash, glitzy world of the silver screen – but, for the public's money, Elizabeth II had all the outward appeal of a Hollywood film-star. With her fine features, lively eye and gleaming smile, she moved in august circles and in the prime of womanhood, exhibiting an impeccable gift for combining popular fashion with the need to dress for the occasion, the poise that comes of years of grooming for the part, modesty in abundance and charm to spare. Add to that a debonair husband who had for five years been the golden boy of the Royal Family, a pigeon pair of delightful children – Charles, serious at three years old, Anne a mischievous toddler – and a doting, indulgent grandmother, widowed at barely fifty years of age, and the picture was complete.

Few could resist marvelling at the comparisons with the young Queen Victoria, the experience of whose long and prosperous reign surely foretold of similar triumphs to come. Somehow this young, vulnerable family seemed to exude the promise of a glorious new Elizabethan age – in which context the death of that magnificent, archetypal Victorian, Queen Mary, just six weeks before Elizabeth's coronation, may have appeared more than symbolic. As we now know, and as the British public learned the hard way, new Elizabethan ages do not arrive merely by being proclaimed. The convictions that came of national wishful thinking in 1953 have been constantly assaulted by Cyprus and Suez, oil crises and economic decline, super-powerdom and terrorism, and the ceaseless, sometimes violent and hard-won struggle for social change.

It was indeed folly to be wise in those early days. The Coronation, for all the economies asked for by the Duke of Edinburgh when he chaired the first meeting of the Coronation Committee, was an extravaganza of a brilliance and on a scale unequalled in living memory. Implicit in its endless gold and silver trappings, its scarlets and purples, its ermines and embroideries, its ancient symbols of kingship and their veiled meanings, was a celebration not only of the best of Britain's colourful heritage, but also a statement of belief in its power to see Britain through any of her national difficulties.

The belief was shared by virtually everyone in that heady Coronation atmosphere, primarily because the entire event was seen on television, and was thus, for the first time, within the witness of a huge proportion of the Queen's admiring subjects. That was made possible thanks only to the Queen herself, for it was she who overruled her Prime Minister, Archbishop of Canterbury and Earl Marshal at a stroke when they advised against allowing the cameras in. It was a perfect example of the monarchy's skilful use of the media for what was effectively publicity purposes. The role of the Crown in history, the relevance of its traditions to its present-day activities, and the function of the monarchy within a democratic society were made visible and explicit against a glorious and memorable backdrop of ancient ceremonial. Its effect on the faithful in Christ was no less salutary. 'The United Kingdom last Tuesday,' said the Archbishop of Canterbury, 'was not very far from the Kingdom of Heaven.' And both the moving homage paid to the young sovereign by her husband, and the appearance of the four-year-old Prince Charles, brought to Westminster Abbey half way through the ceremony to join his aunt and grandmother as they watched from the Royal Gallery, served as reminders that it was not just the Queen, but her family, who were being presented and acclaimed on that day.

A few years of general public goodwill followed, based on that family vision. Everyone, for instance, seemed to share what was widely identified as the poignancy of the royal parents' departure for a six-month Commonwealth tour, involving as it did the necessity of leaving behind two young and impressionable children who had presumably seen precious little of their busy, pre-occupied mother and father in the previous couple of years. During the tour, the nation received, with the oohs and aahs of genuine affection, some officially released photographs showing the two temporary orphans enjoying a weekend with their grandmother at Royal Lodge, her Windsor retreat. And, towards its end, the family reunion – off Tobruk, during the royal visit to Libya – was relished nationally, even internationally, with vicarious emotion and pleasure.

Later there was the enormous interest – indeed thrill – of watching the heir to the Throne attending school in the heart of London, following his parents' decision to send him to public schools in preference to having him educated solely within the walls of Buckingham Palace. There were those delightful incidents during Royal Windsor Horse Shows, Badminton Horse Trials, or Windsor and Cowdray Park polo matches, when the whole family of four could be seen at least in a semblance of relaxation (for it paid, then as now, to be on your guard whenever the press was around): the Queen of England treading down the divots; her husband swinging his polo mallet as if his life depended on it; her children feeding ponies or buying mementoes at side-stalls; all four, plus Grannie and the aunts, uncles and cousins, spread out on rugs and blankets, well wrapped up against Gloucestershire's spring breezes and with only a picket fence separating them from the common herd, all watching horses being put through their paces. It was an idyllic national reverie, and with the profusion of new, colourful magazines and books to record it all, it was rarely other than hot news.

Like most dreams, this one eventually broke. Nineteen-fifty-five had been a disastrous year, ending as it did in the bitter moral confusion following Princess Margaret's renunciation of her suitor of many years, Group-Captain Peter Townsend. Townsend, a former equerry of the Princess' father before being transferred to the household of Queen Elizabeth the Queen Mother, was divorced, and in the high moral and religious atmosphere of the new Elizabethan age, royalty did not marry divorcees. The twenty years since the Abdication had not changed that.

Following a two-year-old simmering of speculation and innuendo in the British press (for the possibility of trouble had been publicly spotted as early as 1953), the story alleging an impending marriage burst into the papers and continued to maintain an unhealthy grip on their readers for six long and distressing months. Scenting, in that prolonged period of official silence, that royalty was on the run, the press became (for those days) openly impertinent, and the headline 'Come on, Margaret: Make up your mind' encapsulated the mood for posterity. Eventually, the Princess was obliged to issue a statement confirming her decision, 'mindful of the Church's teaching that Christian marriage is indissoluble, and conscious of my duty towards the Commonwealth,' not to marry her suitor. Townsend went quietly away to begin a new life.

For the Queen the whole affair was fraught with danger and the threat of dissention and obsessive sensation. She knew that from the beginning, of course, yet tackled it with remarkable calmness and personal sympathy for both her sister and the Group Captain which belied the disturbing possibilities of the case and the anxiety she must have felt. She at first refused to have Townsend banished from the Court – a suggestion put forward by both her Private Secretary and the Prime Minister – then, when her hand was forced at the height of the initial furore, defiantly selected him as her official Equerry-in-Waiting, and was seen chatting freely and amicably to him in public during an official tour of Northern Ireland.

Ultimately she had no constitutional alternative, as Head of the Church of England, to registering and insisting on her formal disapproval of the marriage. Yet it says much for her tact and sense of proportion that the two sisters were then, and have since been, close and appreciative of each other – in spite of the raised eyebrows when Princess Margaret later married Antony Armstrong-Jones, the constant public fixation with the state of that marriage, the distress of the eventual separation and divorce, and the perpetual, intransigent rumours that have dogged the Princess and reflected so badly on the Royal Family since.

As at the Abdication, the public was divided on the rights and wrongs of the Townsend affair, and although it died a decent death as 1956 came round, it soon became apparent that the issues and their treatment in the press had opened up the first questionings of the style of leadership which the Royal Family was adopting. People began to refer in disgruntled fashion to 'the Court' as the element to be criticised for its enduring resistance to change, its outmoded moral and social attitudes, and the consequent aloofness which threatened to alienate the Queen from her subjects. No-one was quite sure who 'the Court' was, but it afforded an acceptable alternative to direct criticism of the sovereign herself – a phenomenon unheard of since the days of Queen Victoria's prolonged mourning back in the 1870s. So without appearing to be disloyal or treasonable – indeed, with every appearance of being thoroughly loyal and protective towards the Queen personally – her critics could assail her advisers for their influences on her, the endless throng of titled hangers-on for sapping the Crown's privileges, and the continuing connection with the faded world of aristocrats (of which the annual presentation of debutantes provided the most glaring example) which had long since ceased to hold the country in thrall.

No sooner had that convenient avenue of hostility been explored than the Queen herself came in for a spate of criticism unparalleled either before or since. Her own childhood awareness of her future role in life had left her with a natural resistance to change and with many of the rather more unfortunate accomplishments of standard royal behaviour which by 1957 was becoming more famous for its anachronistic courtliness than for its relevance to either present or future. In that year, Lord Altrincham vented a sudden and pronounced condemnation of the Queen's personal style in which he described 'the personality conveyed by the utterances put into her mouth' as 'that of a priggish schoolgirl.' The playwright John Osborne had already likened the monarchy to 'the gold filling in the mouth of decay' and had questioned the political value, social relevance and moral stimulus of 'the royal round of gracious boredom, the protocol of ancient fatuity.' As the new editor of *Punch*, Malcolm Muggeridge summarily discontinued that magazine's whimsical and unctuous support of the monarchy as an institution and of the Royal Family as individuals, made his own personal complaints about the Queen's 'dowdy, frumpish' appearance and 'banal' behaviour, deplored the cult of monarchy that had swept the country in the previous ten years and likened its mystical and traditional ceremonies to 'aspirins for a sick society. As a religion, monarchy has always been a failure. A God-King inevitably gets eaten.'

Before 1957 was out, it had become more personal than that. Late the previous year, the Duke of Edinburgh had left Britain for a four-month Commonwealth tour. Not for the first time, he was absent from his wife on their wedding anniversary, and although the Queen took their enforced separation as a theme of her Christmas message – 'My husband's absence at this time has made me even more aware than I was before of my own good fortune in being one of a united family....' – the press began to circulate the tale that not all was well with the royal marriage. Everything from the Duke's repeated absences, to disagreements about the children's education or the organisation of Palace staff was dragged in to support the growing speculation, and a handful of so-called eye-witness accounts from within the Palace – including one which alleged that the Duke had flung a sheaf of papers to his office floor in exasperation after a fruitless conversation with his wife – were cobbled together in an effort to prove it.

Few sensations of this nature have ever lasted long, and a springtime State Visit to Portugal that year seemed tailor-made for at least the appearance of a reconciliation. The Duke travelled to Lisbon direct from Gibraltar, the last port of call of his tour, while the Queen arrived direct from London. The couple were afforded forty minutes' 'private conversation time' inside the Queen's aircraft. As they emerged, one hawk-eyed reporter swore he spotted a little patch of lipstick on the Duke's left cheek, and everyone noticed he was wearing a tie with tiny hearts on it. What better proof could anybody want that the royal rift had been healed? And as if to consolidate the fact, the Queen created her husband a Prince of the United Kingdom – just a hundred years after Queen Victoria created *her* husband Prince Consort.

But the cumulative experience of two difficult years was not lost on the Queen, nor upon the Duke, who was now being credited with making the first steps to 'modernise' the monarchy. By the end of 1958, the debutante presentation parties had ceased in favour of the now famous royal garden parties, to which guests are selected on an immeasurably wider basis. The royal couple began to give monthly Palace luncheons for small groups of public figures – again representing a broad range of activities, from politics to sport and the arts. And the beginnings of greater public exposure occurred with the televising of the Queen's Christmas broadcasts, an illustrated television lecture given by the Duke on his 1956-7 tour, his first BBC interview, and ultimately the televising of State and ceremonial occasions, like Trooping the Colour and the State Opening of Parliament. In her first televised broadcast, the Queen had said, 'It is inevitable that I should seem a rather remote figure to many of you – a successor to the kings and queens of history', but the very occasion showed the flaw in her premise. If there was a feeling of isolation between ruler and ruled, it was no longer inevitable. The Queen's active achievement in bringing the Crown to her subjects dates from this time.

She was undoubtedly helped by the continuous, indeed prodigious family activity which brought the entire institution back into focus and favour after 1959. In August of that year the Queen announced that she was expecting her third child – after a gap of over nine years. The universal surprise at this news, coming at the end of a lengthy trip to Canada in which her health had caused anxiety and spawned mysterious and unsatisfactory official explanations, the fact that this would be the first child born to her as Queen, and the reflection that no baby had been born to a reigning sovereign since Queen Victoria's youngest, Princess Beatrice, over a century before, combined to make the Queen something of a heroine. There was a monumental outburst of patriotism around the Palace gates as her confinement approached, and the eventual news of the birth of a prince gladdened a cold and bleak February. Within the next week, two further events kept the Royal Family in the forefront of public attention – the death of Lady Edwina Mountbatten, and, more significantly, the engagement of Princess Margaret to Antony Armstrong-Jones.

Antony Armstrong-Jones had been a 'society' photographer, appointed by the Royal Family to take official photographs of them for the previous four years or so. His ability to recreate the formality of the Victorian royal photograph (as with the Queen's tenth wedding anniversary pictures in 1957), yet blend dignity with the occasional hint of informality (as with the portraits of Prince Charles and Princess Anne the same year) helped to edge the image of the Queen's immediate family away from the rather fulsome studio effects created by Marcus Adams in earlier decades. He had also taken many of Princess Margaret's birthday portraits during those years, and photographer and sitter had formed a strong, lasting relationship which existed entirely within the privacy of their own, vaguely avant-garde circle. That the announcement, and the Princess' choice of husband, caught the gossip-columnists of the national and international press completely unawares was a tribute to the discretion maintained by the couple's many close friends and associates.

At the same time the engagement did wonders for the process of undoing the Royal Family's remoteness, which the Queen had spoken of back in 1957. Though the genealogists rummaged through their books to discover the bridegroom's royal connections (like his fiancée, he was 23rd in descent from Edward I), there was something rather liberating about the fact that essentially this was a man of commoner origins, without even the shadow of a title in his close ancestry to justify his marriage in the eyes of the diehards. Establishment eyebrows may well have been raised as the guest list was prepared to show a large number of the couple's 'bohemian' friends, noses turned up at wild suggestions that they would start their married life in a flat in Pimlico, and mouths dropped at the realisation that because *his* father had married three times, *she* would have three mothers-in-law. But the truth was that when, on returning into the body of Westminster Abbey after signing the registers, the Princess was described as Mrs Antony Armstrong-Jones, the Royal Family moved a good step closer to every other family in the land.

It was perverse that, when the novelty had worn off, the groom should have been criticised for sponging off the Royal Family and enjoying privileges that most commoners never come within spitting distance of. A costly honeymoon cruise on the *Britannia*, an expensive refurbishment and repair programme to their Kensington Palace apartment, and a place at high table for every State occasion that he could be present at, were all catalysts for the critics. Yet, when he eventually took a permanent job at the Design Centre, then with the *Sunday Times*, he was again taken to task for demeaning the image of his in-laws. His one saving grace was that he did not take a title upon his marriage. That made him very much 'one of us' – until in October 1961, with the birth of his first child only a month away, the Queen bestowed the Earldom of Snowdon upon him. Whether this came at the

Queen's suggestion, or at the new Earl's request, or – as was commonly thought – at the insistence of Princess Margaret because she could not bear to see her children living untitled lives – was never made clear, and perhaps never will be. But it blew part of the legend for ever.

In the meantime the marriage of British royalty with commoners became itself more commonplace. In 1961, the Duke of Kent married Miss Katharine Worsley, the daughter of a North Yorkshire baronet, and two years later the Duke's sister, Princess Alexandra married the Hon Angus Ogilvy, the second son of the Earl of Airlie. And with all three marriages came a spate of royal children. After Prince Andrew's birth in 1960 and that of Viscount Linley the following year, came the birth of the Kents' first child – George, Earl of St Andrews – in 1962. Two years later all four young royal mothers produced children within two months of one another. Princess Alexandra's son James came first (on Leap Year's Day), the Queen's third son, Prince Edward, followed ten days later; then the Duchess of Kent's daughter, Lady Helen Windsor, arrived at the end of April, three days before Princess Margaret's daughter, Lady Sarah Armstrong-Jones, on May Day. The Year of the Royal Babies, as it became known, was the climax of a four-year period that saw the number of royal children of Prince Charles' generation increase from two to nine (eleven if you count two others born out of wedlock to the Harewood brothers – but that's another story).

It also saw the end of another period of intense interest in, and immense popularity for, the Royal Family. Three years passed by which were relatively quiet in terms of publicity, highlighted only by such events as the State Funeral of Sir Winston Churchill, the Queen's first State Visit to West Germany, the launching of the *QEII* and some lengthy Commonwealth tours. It was during this comparatively low-profile period that the Queen addressed herself to one particularly delicate family matter. For over thirty years the Duke and Duchess of Windsor had been virtual outcasts of the family whose name they bore. Since the Duke's voluntary exile in 1936, he and his wife had been infrequent and irregular visitors to Britain, prompted to return here only by urgent family and national matters – the outbreak of War in 1939, a meeting with Queen Mary in 1945, the funeral of King George VI in 1952, and so on.

In 1965, the Duke and Duchess came to London where the Duke underwent medical treatment to one of his eyes. The Queen took the opportunity to call in on him at his hotel, Claridge's, and spend an hour or so talking with both him and the Duchess. It was a private meeting, but publicly acknowledged, and it created great speculation that the Abdication, its cause and effect, would all be forgiven if not forgotten. It certainly looked as if the frequent public outcries against the Royal Family's apparent indifference or incivility towards the Windsors was having an effect, and that this visit was the Queen's way of showing that private relations between them were not as bad as everyone seemed to think.

Two years later the Windsors were back in London again, this time by virtue of a royal invitation to a public ceremony. Nineteen-sixty-seven was the centenary year of the birth of Queen Mary, and her grand-daughter was to unveil a plaque to her memory in the wall of Marlborough House, the old Queen's London residence for the last eight years of her life. It would indeed have been churlish and unforgiveable if the Duke had not been invited to attend the unveiling, but few people might have expected the invitation to extend to the Duchess. Queen Mary herself was implacably opposed to the former Mrs Simpson, and right up to her death could bring herself to no point of reconciliation beyond that of adding a postscript to one of her letters to her son which read, ' 'I send a kind message to your wife.' It was and is strongly believed that Queen Elizabeth the Queen Mother was at least as firmly opposed to the Duchess of Windsor's being received at Court or accorded any treatment implying her acceptance into the family. But other contemporaries, notably the then Duke and Duchess of Gloucester and Princess Marina, had visited the Windsors in the past, while the younger generation in the persons of Prince Charles and Princess Alexandra had more recently paid their respects when in Paris. The Queen clearly decided that her most senior aunt's continued exclusion from the family could no longer be justified, and that she should therefore be invited to join the Duke at Marlborough House. Which she did, thus ending in full public view a spiritual as well as physical exile which had lasted three decades. She was then in her seventy-first year.

Five years later, the Queen was in Paris on her second State Visit to France. At short notice, and much to the interest of royal-watchers on both sides of the Channel, a brief visit to the Windsors' house in the Bois de Boulogne was included in the royal schedule. The undisclosed reason for this late change to a programme agreed weeks before spawned widespread speculation. More gratuitous goodwill on both sides? Another public display of reconciliation? The chance of a home for the Windsors in Britain? The Duchess to become Her Royal Highness as last? A hint of the answer came with the news that the Duke was not well enough to greet his niece, and could meet her only in his room. After the meeting, only the Duchess came outside to see the Queen, Prince Philip and Prince Charles leave. The royal smiles, and even the Duchess' pained, fixed pursing of the lips hid for the moment the fact that the Duke's days were numbered. He would lie on his death-bed for no more than eight more days before finally succumbing to advanced cancer of the throat.

Apart from the Duchess' brief stay at Buckingham Palace for the Duke's obsequies, there seemed no reconciliation even in death. The body of the Duke was interred at Frogmore after a Lying-in-State at Windsor, all in accordance with his wishes. The Duchess, who directly after his funeral left Britain for the last time, and unaccompanied by any member of her dead husband's family, still has no home in his country. Now in her nineties, she will, when her distressing, prolonged and weary senility is finally ended, lie beside him in those royal grounds.

This long-running royal controversy may well have seemed a world away from the bright promise which the younger generation of the Royal Family offered back in 1967. In that year Prince Charles completed his five-year secondary education at Gordonstoun, the Scotland-based school which his father had attended and to which both his brothers were to follow him, and went up to Cambridge to begin a three-year degree course in history, archaeology and anthropology. The choice of these heavily academic subjects disappointed many people for whom they implied that the student himself would be a dull, possibly pedantic plodder. In a sense, that reaction proved how little was known about him at the time, and thus how well the Queen had managed to keep her son out of the public eye since he first trotted off to school in 1957.

It was not long before the Prince showed his true colours. From the modest, reserved boy he had always seemed to be, he emerged, long before the end of his first year at Cambridge, as a sensible, thoughtful student with a personable nature and a refreshing, slightly zany, sense of humour. The popular suspicions that, for all the Queen's attempts to bring him up as normally as possible, he would turn out as a ready-made king-to-be, processed out of Establishment material from the inner sanctums of Buckingham Palace, were quickly dispelled as he threw himself into the University's social, as well as academic, life. It was at Cambridge that he developed his musical talents, learning to play the trumpet (until one of his orchestral colleagues couldn't stand the sound he was making), and subsequently taking up the cello. He became an active member of the University's Dryden Dramatic Society, and was soon famous as a man of many parts, playing the roles of dustmen, vicars, lechers and spoilt aristocrats with equal adroitness, displaying his long-standing and recently disclosed affection for the crazy humour of the Goons, and, most important of all, able and willing to allow some of his audience's laughter to be turned against himself. 'Were it not for my ability to see the funny side of my life,' he once said, 'I'd have been committed to an institution long ago.'

As it happened, the emergence of this side of the Prince's character, its relative openness, frankness and – despite his having been brought up very much in the company of older people – refreshing youthfulness, provided the impetus for the next stage in the monarchy's move towards closer identification with its subjects. Back in 1958, the Queen had created her son Prince of Wales and promised to present him to the Welsh people at Caernarfon 'when he is grown up.' A decade later she decided that 1969 would be the year in which this ceremonial presentation would be acted out, and in the year-long run-up to the event she approved a monumental publicity exercise (not to put too fine a point on it) which broke so many shackles with the restrictive practices of the past that to all public appearances the Royal Family has never been the same since.

By and large, the idea was to drive home the fact that the Queen and her growing family were, at heart, no more than human, like everybody else. To put the idea across, she authorised the production of a blockbusting television film documentary, called simply *Royal Family*, in which the cameras were allowed to film the Queen and her relations at work and at play. The Queen was seen in her office at Buckingham Palace, scrutinising draft speeches, choosing jewellery for the next State Visit, and approving a new set of postage stamps; Prince Philip was shown discussing with his staff the logistics of travel in order to squeeze as many engagements into a day as possible, then climbing into a helicopter in the grounds of the Palace; Prince Charles was seen bicycling round Cambridge, shopping for provisions, and making shift for himself in his rooms; Princess Anne was filmed during a lesson at the Berlitz School of Languages where she was undergoing a course in French. Of the younger children, Prince Andrew was playing football at his school in Berkshire, while Prince Edward, then only five, shared a lesson in the Buckingham Palace schoolroom with his cousins and close friends.

On the purely official side there were inside shots for the very first time of a royal Investiture, and of the Queen giving numerous audiences to ambassadors, High Commissioners, foreign heads of state (including President Nixon), and heads of Commonwealth governments. She was seen hosting a Buckingham Palace garden party, the annual Diplomatic Reception, and a less formal, but no less well-attended, Palace reception for the British Olympic team, and carrying out her outside duties in Britain and during her 1968 State Visit to South America. It was a fascinating (if, for obvious reasons, not totally complete) insight into the workings of monarchy, and brought home the fact that an enormous amount of hard graft and thought behind the scenes goes into the work of a sovereign, which most people see as only a superficial, rather easy job where everything runs smoothly and predictably.

But most important of all, the film achieved its main objective of projecting the Royal Family as a family of individuals with the attributes (if not the lifestyle) of ordinary human beings. It disproved the falsehoods that they never eat together, or that they never do anything for themselves, or that they have equerries and ladies-in-waiting around them wherever they go. Here was film of Prince Charles whizzing around a Windsor Castle courtyard in a go-kart, of Prince Edward being rowed across a Scottish lake by his father, of Prince Andrew snowballing with his younger brother at Sandringham, of Prince Philip painting a water-colour at Windsor. Here was the whole family enjoying a barbecue on the Balmoral estate, with the Queen helping Prince Charles to mix the salad dressing, the Duke and Princess Anne grilling sausages and steaks. Here they were chatting casually at the lunch table at Buckingham Palace, swopping stories about everything from King George VI's temper to hilarious incidents during state visits. Here was the Queen and Prince Philip travelling by air from one engagement to another – *he* putting the finishing touches to a speech, *she* reading *The Sporting Life* to keep up with the latest racing developments. And here was the whole family – sisters, cousins and aunts – sharing Christmas at Windsor; the Queen's four children helping to dress a huge Christmas tree, the Snowdons' children picking out their favourite ancestral portraits under the benign eye of the Queen Mother, the young Kent cousins all dressed up in smart white woollies and bobble hats, ready for outdoor games, and the Ogilvy children ploughing down the corridors in their toy cars, followed by Princess Alexandra pushing a trolley laden with presents.

And so it went on. The film, shown only days before Prince Charles' Investiture, was rapturously received, watched by almost 75% of Britain's population, and clamoured for by the rest of the Western world. It made the Investiture itself – a modernised ceremony, yet packed full of ancient ritual and sonority – somehow surprisingly relevant, where otherwise it may have seemed a mere dressing-up charade with king, queen, jacks, jokers and all. And without doubt it ushered in the new royal generation, and paved the way for the style its young representatives would adopt if the monarchy were to be made as relevant to the 21st century as it had been in the twentieth.

Setting the pace for this renaissance were Prince Charles himself and his sister Princess Anne. The Prince continued to busy himself at Cambridge, which he left with a History degree in 1970 to take up a naval career for the following six years. In that time he combined his service duties with a wide range of official programmes, dispensing independence to various Commonwealth countries, representing the Queen at foreign coronations and the funerals of heads of state, and touring the world both with and without his parents. In those kinds of capacities he was seen far and wide, in a variety of new, colourful and appealing locations, trying his hand at a whole range of new experiences. And unlike his mother before him, he felt able – possibly obliged – to take part actively in whatever amusement or diversion was offered to him. The Queen would never climb a ladder, wield a snooker cue, pick up a child, dive into a crowd, or press any button unless the consequence was absolutely guaranteed. Prince Charles, even in those early years, seemed irresistibly drawn to that very kind of behaviour. He crawled into igloos, walked upside-down on the underside of Arctic ice, rode camels, performed love-dances in Fiji, dressed up in Ghanaian tribal chiefs' robes, smoked peace-pipes in Canada, and was more than once on the receiving end of custard pies.

Princess Anne undertook her first solo engagement at the age of eighteen, and lost no time in making her own impact on a curious and receptive public. Her two strengths were her flair for colourful clothes and penchant for eye-catching hats, and her forthright manner which, at the occasional risk of appearing brusque, reminded everyone much more of her father than of her mother. In the four years before her marriage, her impressive wardrobe of clothes made her by far the most talked-about and sought-after member of the Royal Family. She made a point of buying British, choosing frequently off the peg, and patronising the departmental stores rather than the standard Palace couturiers and fashion houses. In her choice of day clothes she took fullest advantage of the trend towards stunning, vivid colours, and appeared in emerald greens, peacock blues, shocking pinks, tomato reds and sunshine yellows with a regularity and predictability that made her a standard target for any press photographer wishing to stay in work. Her evening dresses were little short of magnificent: with her mature eye for style with dignity, her love of shimmering colour, and her dazzling collection of personal jewellery, she outshone all around her to such a degree that she was frequently accused of having upstaged the Queen herself. She often denied that she had any appreciable eye for fashion, shrugged off the 'swinging princess' label that had been tagged onto her, and even once protested that she thought herself rather staid. But her wide-brimmed hats, trouser-suits, mini-skirts and squat-heeled shoes echoed the burgeoning youthfulness of the times and may have done more than anyone realised to maintain that ethereal relationship between Crown and people that, rightly or wrongly, depends these days as much upon surface trivia as upon deep-rooted respect for tradition and matriarchy.

If the delicacy of that relationship was ever in doubt, it was illustrated by Princess Anne's other quality – the honesty of approach and reaction that suffers no fool gladly, and (to use phraseology of which she would approve) lets one know exactly where one stands. She once told the Americans that a bald eagle for their national symbol was 'a rather bad choice', insisted that she was delighted she never had a sister, condemned tennis as 'far too gladiatorial', complained that she would never get a good career, and warned all and sundry that 'I don't enjoy being pushed and shoved around by other people.' She has openly admitted not being 'much enamoured of London', and has condemned smokers, drinkers, people who make long speeches, and those who serve her exotic food. Her tirades against the press soon became as legendary as they were successively controversial. No Badminton or Burghley was complete in the early 1970s without a volley of protest from competitor HRH Princess Anne which usually ended with a choice phrase from her substantial armoury of maledictions. 'Go Away', 'Clear Out', 'Get Lost' and 'Shove Off' all became respectable through constant and well-reported royal usage.

In many ways, this honest and unbridled show of independence and self-respect rebounded upon her. 'Who learned Princess Anne to swear?' asked one five-year-old child once. The point was not lost on the Princess, who herself admitted that 'when I appear in public, people expect me to neigh, grind my teeth, paw the ground and swish my tail.' But her behaviour, and the courage she showed in exhibiting it, won her many admirers. Even her critics came eventually to see her side of a controversy which was often reported one-sidedly by her main victims, the press. 'You tend to be rather a touchy lot, too,' she chided them once, and they didn't disagree. What was more, she proved to be one of the first to give the lie to the belief that royalty cannot answer back. In many respects it still can't, but there are limits even to royal patience at times, and these days you get no credit for reining in your tongue when to do the opposite would be everyone else's natural reaction.

Ever since her official launching onto the public scene, Princess Anne had been carefully watched by the press and public for signs that she would marry. The opportunities for speculation were very limited. Her sole recreational interest appeared to be in the horse world and, as she herself admitted, never with the sophisticated night-club life that had so attracted her aunt Princess Margaret and her great uncle Edward VIII. And her equestrian involvement was total and uncompromising, a constant and progressive effort that stopped at nothing short of the excellence that eventually won her the European Championship in 1971. It seemed that her frequent and unconcealed meetings and conversations with male companions from the world of eventing and show-jumping – notably Richard Meade and Andrew Parker-Bowles – were too obvious to carry romantic connotations, and it was consequently a long time before the companionship of one Lieut. Mark Phillips was seized upon by the press as being anything other than platonic. By the end of 1972, Lieut. Phillips had proved himself an excellent horseman, with two Badminton championships to his credit and a clutch of honours from his participation in British teams for successive European, Olympic and World Championships.

He had also proved himself to be a prime contender for the hand of the Queen's daughter, the public assumption of which was strengthened by the many sightings the following spring of the Princess and the Lieutenant training and exercising their horses together in preparation for the eventing season to come. More than once they faced a bevy of photographers in the middle of these training sessions, and more than once Princess Anne issued her authoritative and quick-tempered denials that there was anything more between them than a love of horses. Only after the 1973 Badminton – in which Princess Anne finished eighth and Mark finished up in the lake – did the tone of her responses soften and their appearances together become more circumspectly arranged. By the end of May they were engaged. By the end of the year they were married.

The marriage of members of the Royal Family, particularly where romance has been long suspected and denied, is often followed by a falling off of public interest, as if each wedding were the culmination of a particular story. To an extent this was true of Princess Anne, though their claim to popular attention was momentarily revived early in 1974 after a gunman tried to kidnap her, and the following year when Gatcombe Park was purchased for her and her husband by the Queen. Certainly Prince Philip had been aware of how easily established members of the Royal Family can be lost sight of. Back in the 1960s he admitted that he and the Queen were entering a stage of life at which the glamour has worn off – and he was right. With popular interest focused strongly on their two elder children, the Queen and her husband spent much of the 1970s in comparative shade, maintaining a regular and conscientious work schedule that only rarely produced anything totally new or spectacular.

There was no conscious effort to counter this inevitable shift in popularity, and it would have been wrong for it to be otherwise. Nevertheless. one of the main highlights of the decade was centred upon the Queen and Prince Philip, not only as individuals, but also as the senior members of a nation's surrogate family. This was very much a family affair – the Silver Wedding celebrations in November 1972, marked by a thanksgiving service in Westminster Abbey and a Lord Mayoral luncheon at the Guildhall. It was at this luncheon that the Queen reaffirmed her personal commitment to the sanctity of the family unit, speaking of the relationship between man and wife as capable of maturity and development only if it is 'held firm in the web of family relationships between parents and children, grandparents and grandchildren, cousins, aunts and uncles.'

To commemorate the event for posterity, and almost as if to reinforce the Queen's sentiments, the royal couple had a wealth of photographs officially released, many of which were taken at and around Balmoral during the previous summer holidays. Some of these pictures depicted all four of their children, as indeed did a later portfolio of photographs, taken on the wedding anniversary itself, in which congratulatory telegrams were being opened and relished.

But more significant for the perpetuation of that all-important family image was the set of pictures taken by the Queen Mother's nephew, Lord Lichfield, in which most of the surviving representatives of the families of King George V's children were shown. With the Queen's immediate family were the Queen Mother, Princess Margaret and Lord Snowdon with their children, the Duke and Duchess of Kent with theirs (including the two-year-old Lord Nicholas Windsor), the bachelor Prince Michael, and Princess Alexandra and her family. Only the Harewoods, the two sons of the late Princess Royal, were missing, presumably by reason of their untoward history of extra-marital relationships, and the Gloucesters, for whom the early 1970s was a particularly tragic time.

Despite its comparative seniority, the Gloucester family has always preferred to exist in the shadows of publicity. By nature a shy man, the old Duke of Gloucester was a dutiful and reliable, if unimaginative, royal who enjoyed nothing better than the straightforward private life of a securely-based aristocrat. Country pleasures and the company of tried and trusted friends were all he asked, and in this he found a perfect companion in his wife. They had two children, though quite late in life, and at the temporary expense of the Duchess' health and several miscarriages. In 1967 the Duke suffered a stroke which left him badly paralysed and virtually speechless. His wife took on a large proportion of the duties in respect of which he was in receipt of Civil List payments, and their elder son Prince William was made aware that his chosen diplomatic career would have to come to an end rather sooner that had otherwise been expected.

By that frustrating irony which afflicts the Royal Family as much as anyone, it was Prince William who died first. A fanatic for speed and adventure, he entered himself for an air race at Wolverhampton in August, 1972. His plane had hardly left the ground before it turned, banked steeply, lost height and crashed to the ground in flames. The news of his instant death, brought to his seventy-year-old mother by another competitor, numbed her beyond grief. Coupled with the difficult and distressing anguish of caring for her invalid and virtually helpless husband during the two further years that preceded his death, the experience persuaded her that she should retire from public life altogether.

It says much for the Royal Family's sense of duty that she allowed her decision to be reversed. Her younger son, Prince Richard, and the Danish born Birgitte van Deurs whom he had married only seven weeks before Prince William died, took on full-time duties as the new Duke and Duchess of Gloucester, while the widowed Duchess, now known as Princess Alice, found it impossible to loose herself from the many enjoyable associations she had made during her forty years as a member of the Royal Family. At the time of her eightieth birthday, she resolved again to reduce the numbers of her public engagements, but again without success. 'The trouble is,' she explained, 'that when you have been associated with organisations for so many years, and they plead with you to do something again that you did for them last year, or say it's all going to be a terrible flop if you don't go, what can you do?'

And so, half-way through her eighties, she goes on. She is now the proud grandmother of three youngsters – Alexander, Earl of Ulster, born in 1974, and Ladies Davina and Rose Windsor, born in 1977 and 1980 respectively. She has certainly appreciated the truth of the Queen's perception of the importance of the family, as expressed in that Silver Wedding speech. Though, even as she spoke those words, the Queen herself must have been aware of the irony of her remarks. For at that very time the marriage of her sister, Princess Margaret, and Lord Snowdon was going through a traumatic stage of bitterness and indifference from which it was never to recover. The whys and wherefores of the growing estrangement, and the rights and wrongs of the case, are still the subject of debate and dispute, and blame has been variously apportioned ever since by all manner of people claiming to have been in the know. What is clear is that rumours of family rows, sudden absences and alleged affairs had been mounting steadily for several years and that Lord Snowdon was being seen less and less frequently in the company of his wife as the 1970s wore on. Thus the announcement, early in 1976, that the Princess and her husband were to separate came as no great surprise and, as if there were some kind of universal relief that the tension of so many years' speculation had been released at last, the couple were left to live out the two-year period before their inevitable divorce in relative peace and privacy. In 1978 the Princess obtained a dissolution of the marriage under what is glibly called the 'quickie' system, by which the High Court may grant an instant divorce on mutually agreed evidence that the parties have lived apart for two years and consider the breakdown of their marriage to be irreconcilable.

Conversely, and not without its own hint of irony, another royal romance was on the horizon, with not only divorce but also religion among its potential hazards. Prince Michael of Kent, whose elder brother and sister had each married in the early 1960s, had formed a tenacious and well-publicised attachment with the former Baroness Marie-Christine von Reibnitz, a Czech-born lady of aristocratic antecedents whose marriage to a Mr Thomas Troubridge had already effectively broken down. It was well-known by the beginning of 1978 (when Princess Margaret's marriage was nearing its own end) that Prince Michael was waiting only for the Troubridge union to be annulled before he could go to the Queen and request her consent to wed Marie-Christine. In the more liberated atmosphere of the times (the Earl of Harewood had remarried following his divorce in 1967, and his brother was about to follow suit), and with Prince Michael being sixteenth in the line of succession, the Queen's consent would not have been difficult to give, but the fact that the lady was a Roman Catholic posed constitutional problems which it was not within the Queen's power to ignore.

The outcome effectively relegated the ghost of the Abdication controversy, to which it was likened, to the history books. The Baroness' annulment proved no bar to the Queen's permission for the Prince to marry her, and any religious objection was overcome by the simple expedient of Prince Michael's renunciation of his purely academic right of succession. It was not much to give up for the prospect of a lifetime's happiness, particularly as the renunciation did not extend to the couple's children. Indeed, the circumstances of the romance (which culminated in a Viennese wedding in June, 1978) raised Marie-Christine almost embarrassingly high in public esteem. She proved more than worthy of the accolade. High-spirited, yet of regal bearing, cultivated, colourful and considerate, she seemed to require no instruction on how to walk with kings nor lose the common touch. Despite, possibly because of, the persistent journalistic knifings she suffered at the hands of one gossip columnist in particular, she has been immensely popular and her presence in public is highly sought after. Her long and determined battle to win Papal recognition for her second marriage was blessed with success after five years of effort and uncertainty, and she came through the appalling opprobrium which followed the revelation of her father's membership of the German SS during the War with a humility and dignity that begged no forgiveness yet won universal sympathy.

The major royal events of the late 1970s might well have suggested that the fierce glare of publicity had shifted back from the younger to the older generations of the Royal Family. The Queen's Silver Jubilee of 1977 was certainly another indication that in spite of the appeal of youth, a national sentiment and goodwill still existed in favour of those with a proven royal record – and in this of all years, the Queen was the epitome of reliability and accumulated wisdom. She had already reigned longer than two-thirds of her predecessors since the Norman Conquest, and although initially there was, in the adverse economic and social climate, little national appetite for a full-blown celebration of what was, after all, an anniversary of a purely arbitrary significance in time, the feeling gained momentum that throughout a quarter century of enormous, unprecedented and often bewildering change, the Queen remained the one constant factor. Older and staider she might be – certainly she had lost, gracefully and imperceptibly, the polished bloom and vivacity of her early womanhood – but she was as dedicated as ever, still smiling despite the little personal troubles, family problems and occasional constitutional storms which she had been obliged to weather.

And, of course, as the official celebrations confirmed, she had around her a huge family which, for all its diversity of age, seniority, interests and lifestyle, was probably more tightly united that most in Britain. Prince Philip was, at 55, still prolonging and extending his associations with such organisations as the World Wildlife Fund, the Duke of Edinburgh's Award Scheme and the Royal Yacht Squadron, and remained the Royal Family's mouthpiece on all manner of subjects regardless of their controversial implications. Prince Charles, then nearing thirty, had proved a good all-rounder, absorbing his experiences as heir to the throne more widely and deeply than any of his predecessors. Princess Anne, a 27-year-old mother-to-be, was acquiring a reputation as a committed and indefatigable worker for prime good causes such as the Save The Children Fund and the Riding for the Disabled Association. Prince Andrew was approaching his constitutional majority and a twelve-year career in the Royal Navy, while his younger brother, 14-year-old Prince Edward, remained very much an unknown quantity, enjoying a more complete degree of personal privacy than any of his siblings before him.

Beyond the Queen's immediate family, Princess Margaret pursued her royal duties with an emphasis on the arts, while her estranged husband busied himself with a host a photographic projects which took him all over the world. Their children were still at school – Bedales on the Hampshire/Sussex borders – and thus not yet within sight of the careers that would make a woodwork designer out of Viscount Linley, and Lady Sarah an art student. Then came the three generations of the Gloucesters, a quiet, dependable family devoted to its own thriving farming business in Northamptonshire when not on royal call; and finally the growing Kent clan.

The Duke and Duchess of Kent's three children grew apace: young George was at Eton, revelling in the beginnings of a brilliantly successful education that would eventually send him to Cambridge and earn him the reputation of being the brainiest member of the Royal Family; his sister Helen was already supporting the long-held theory that the females of the Kent family had, ever since Princess Marina married Prince George in 1934, been easily the most attractive of all in the Royal Family – though it was some years before birthday portraits by Lord Snowdon and Tim Graham would show her to be not only superbly photogenic but also quite exceptionally lovely.

George and Helen's younger brother Nicholas was seven years old in Jubilee year. Born over six years after his sister, he was considered very much a 'late addition' to the family, though in fact there was hope for an even later addition when the Duchess of Kent fell pregnant again in mid-1977. Unhappily, though perhaps not surprisingly, for she was then almost 45 years of age, she was rushed to hospital in late October where she suffered a miscarriage. Though she seemed to overcome the physical and psychological strains of that pregnancy and its outcome, the distress signalled a six-year period of health problems for the Duchess, whose chief attribute with her public was her deep, uninhibited, caring and very personal involvement with the handicapped, the sick and the dying. The successive health crises in her own life until 1983 brought her and her family into a prominence quite disproportionate to their position in the line of succession, as well as unsought by and distasteful to them personally.

The Ogilvies – the most junior-ranking branch of the Kent family - were luckier in their quest for the quiet life, which they successfully secured until threatened by the taint of scandal in the wake of the Lonrho affair during Jubilee year itself. Back in 1973, a series of allegations concerning the activities of some of the directors of the international company Lonrho – of which Mr Ogilvy was one – rocked the business world and even elicited the public condemnation of the Prime Minister, Edward Heath. Wisely, Mr Ogilvy resigned his directorship, along with fifty or so other similar posts which he had acquired long before his marriage to the Princess in 1963. By 1977, and in the belief of exoneration, he had begun to re-acquire directorships, but the story gained credence, against the hottest public denials, that criminal charges against him were being considered by the Director of Public Prosecutions. Any such prospective action came to nothing. Princess Alexandra continues now, as she did then, to fulfil the modest supporting role that has been hers since she reached the age of eighteen in 1954. Her husband, despite recurrent health problems affecting his back and his eyesight, maintains his City associations and his interest in art through his directorship of Sotheby's. Their children, James and Marina, aged 13 and nine respectively in Jubilee year, followed a quiet, uninterrupted lifestyle of which their cousins in Buckingham Palace might have been more than a little envious.

Though the Queen stood at the head of this expanding family, there were others around her whom she might well have considered not only older, but also wiser than she, and in many respects the following years – especially from 1979 to 1981 – were memorable in connection with them, and arguably with them alone. In August 1979 (almost on the very anniversaries of the death of Prince George, Duke of Kent on active service in 1942, and of Prince William of Gloucester in 1972), Lord Mountbatten was killed when the fishing boat he was sailing in was blown up by the IRA off the north-west coast of Ireland. In that split second, Prince Philip lost an uncle and surrogate father, the Queen lost a valued adviser, Prince Charles lost a mentor to whom he was unashamedly devoted, and the Royal Family lost a man who, for all his vanity and persistence on behalf of himself and the name of Mountbatten, was probably at the root of the triumph of survival and popularity in which the monarchy could at that very moment justifiably bask. He was in his eightieth year at the time of his deplorable murder, and posed no conceivable threat to the IRA or their cause. He had pursued a remarkable career in the Royal Navy; had avenged the execration unjustly heaped on his German-born father during World War 1 by assuming, decades later, his mantle of First Sea Lord; had contracted a brilliant, if sometimes tumultuous marriage; and had overseen the problematical and dangerous transition of India from imperial dominion to independent, though divided, nation. After such an active and successful life, it might have been argued that the fading and debilitating years of extreme old age would not have been for him. Yet the manner of his death horrified the world, and the sheer disbelief it prompted among those least conscious of or touched by his many achievements testified to the mute realisation that in this so-called civilised century, unspeakable dangers lurked even for the least influential of public figures, and that being royal was certainly no guarantee of exemption from peril.

Lord Mountbatten was as exact a contemporary as you could wish to find of that other long-established royal figure, Queen Elizabeth the Queen Mother – indeed they were born within six weeks of each other in the dying months of Queen Victoria's long reign. It seemed a cruel stroke of fate that deprived Mountbatten of being associated in 1980 with the warm and appreciative celebration of the Queen Mother's eightieth birthday. Though it involved a glowing service of thanksgiving in St Paul's Cathedral, elegant processions of landaus and princes on horseback, a balcony appearance, and official photographs before and on the chosen day, it was no formal State occasion, but rather a pleasant mid-summer jubilee for a much-loved grannie figure. Since her widowhood almost thirty years before, the Queen Mother had gone about her private and public business with that sense of purpose which was the foundation of her strong character, but at the same time in the knowledge that, because the reins of constitutional power lay with her daughter, many of her own coming and goings must remain comparatively unsung, if not exactly unheralded. For all that she revels in a little bit of fuss – and she certainly got it on that July day in 1980 – the Queen Mother has since 1952 been resigned to taking second place, even if she may occasionally reflect that fate cheated her of the full reward of those long years of dedication and anxiety when the Crown and the country were successively in a less secure condition.

With all the plaudits she received as she entered her octagenarian years, she might well have felt justified in calling a halt to her 57 years of public service. Indeed, for some time beforehand the number of her engagements had been dwindling. Time has, however, proved anyone wrong who thought retirement near. The ghost of Queen Mary, who did not consider one's duty fully accomplished with the coming of any birthday, no matter how advanced, seems still to haunt the royal palaces and keep their occupants up to the mark. So her successor as Queen Consort and dowager has now passed the half-way mark to her nineties, and is still going strong. Tolerant of modern trends and fashions yet resolutely loyal to her own, selective of acquaintance and fast of friendship, an inspiration in her time to all four of her grandchildren, bothered only occasionally by illness, notoriously unpunctual, a warm and sincere speaker, a vintage charmer with time and patience to spare, she has probably never enjoyed life so much as she does now. And on June 3rd, 1986, she became the longest lived Queen Consort in British history.

But not quite the oldest member of the Royal Family – yet. That distinction belonged to Princess Alice, Countess of Athlone who died at the beginning of 1981, within seven weeks of her 98th birthday. The daughter of the haemophiliac Prince Leopold, youngest son of Queen Victoria, Princess Alice gave her only television interview in 1975, at the age of 93, and painted a fascinating picture of her early life at Court – when the ageing Queen used to dispense gold sovereigns from a coral and gold bag for every tooth her grandchildren could claim to have lost; when the family visited Germany and were subjected to the Kaiser's pompous, stiff hospitality; when Alice's brother was sick in the royal carriage during Queen Victoria's Diamond Jubilee procession; and when the Queen's funeral horses refused to pull her hearse and had to be replaced with a contingent of naval cadets. In those days, she said, every member of the family was expected to behave with the utmost decorum and correctness. 'People are watching,' she was told. 'You're doing this for the Queen.'

In essence, things have changed little in the nine decades that have followed. People are still watching, though with less insistence on those impeccable, stiff-upper-lip niceties that nowadays make Victorian standards of behaviour appear faintly ridiculous. And the Royal Family are still doing this, that and the other thing, very much for the Queen.

On the day before what would have been Princess Alice's 98th birthday, Prince Charles announced his engagement to Lady Diana Spencer. The wedding that took place the following July may not have been quite the equal of Queen Victoria's Diamond Jubilee service, but for the 750 million people watching the ceremony and celebrations world-wide, it may not have fallen far short. The story of the Royal Family continues with this young couple and their two delightful children shaping up to the prospect of Prince Charles' kingship and all that it entails for them personally and for those many royal relatives who will be expected to maintain their supporting roles for the future Charles III as they are doing for Elizabeth II.

The last five years of that story unfolds in the following pages, in the blaze of colour which sets royal events and personalities apart from the routine daily round which the rest of us tolerate with or without cheerfulness. If that one truth should jar, remember that, for all their privileges – from the untaxed wealth to the opportunity to travel the world almost at the touch of a button – the Queen and her family have responsibilities which are not only official but also uncomfortably personal. If you have ever said you wouldn't have their job for all the tea in China, you may have been reflecting that there may be more than a few disadvantages in a lifestyle which prevents you from remaining anonymous in a crowd, or being truly alone within your own four security-surrounded walls, or doing what you like, when you like, how you like. Hopping on a bus, spending real money, and not knowing quite what's round the corner may be considered positive freedoms when we realise that, unlike them, we can do all these things without having to watch for sneak photographers, confer with ubiquitous equerries and advisors, consult time-schedules, map out our lives in detail for at least two years in advance, maintain a permanent toothpaste smile and keep the conversation going at all costs. Rather them than me? It's a sobering thought.

Where to begin and end any account of a year in the life of the British Royal Family? It is tempting to plump for the calendar year as the safest and most easily recognisable period, but the long and unashamedly leisurely royal vacation at Balmoral provides cogent evidence that the Queen at least sees her public year as starting in October and finishing the following July. There is a case for treating the Queen's official birthday, traditionally celebrated on the second Saturday in June, as the event which divides one year from the next: this was indeed the basis on which the one and only comprehensive and authorised film about a typical royal year – *Royal Family,* shown in the run-up to the Investiture of Prince Charles as Prince of Wales in July 1969 – was produced.

A fixed event like Trooping the

organisers for whom this is truly a once-a-year occasion; the stall-holders whose harvest of customers must be attracted to what they have to sell; the fairground which makes a mint of money out of the fact that the Derby has long since become a family occasion on which children have to be catered for as fully as their parents.

The nervous tension belongs, and is the prerogative of, the small army of owners, trainers, stable-lads, grooms and, by no means least of all, the jockeys. For all of them, an enterprise which began as much as four years before, when the sires and dams of today's runners were mated almost specifically with this occasion in mind, comes to fruition. The result of the race determines not only the destination of over £200,000 worth of prize money, but also the stud value of every horse

Colour is probably the best candidate of the three, punctuating the year as it does with the unchanging and normally triumphant celebration of a royal tribute by a resplendent militia in full ceremonial dress. Equally unchanging is the annual Derby meeting. Epsom in early June of 1981 provided a major

focal point, even for just one afternoon, for so many people – royalty and commoners, British and foreign, sporting and spectating, serious-minded and fun-seeking – and we have chosen that event to begin our chronicle of five years of colourful happenings, both local, national and international, over which the Queen, as Head of

State, and her family in its supporting role have presided. The Derby, held every year on Epsom Downs, has never lost its grip on the public imagination. Off the course and outside the specialised and highly commercial confines of the world of thoroughbred breeding, the event attracts the speculation of millions of ordinary men and women, who on this occasion as on no other sink many more millions of pounds into what is sometimes, if a little unkindly, called the bookmakers' benevolent fund.

On and around the course, the day itself is one of feverish activity and tensed nerves. The feverish activity is that of the

taking part. A victory at this most especial of Britain's five Classic races puts the winner into such demand as a stallion, that £10 million is these days a cheap price to pay for him.

The Queen, seeking the first Derby win for a member of her family in over three quarters of a century, declared her own entry, which she does as often as not. His name was Church Parade and the Queen's reservations about his chances of success seemed to be evidenced by the fleeting, uncertain looks on her normally relaxed features as the proceedings got under way on 3rd June. Appearances had to be kept up, however, and she arrived, accompanied by the

Queen Mother (opposite page, top), smiling brightly as the motorcade crept silently up the course.

Fashion-wise, 1981 seemed to be the year in which deep, bright colours took the place of paler shades and subtle pastels, as the Queen was obviously aware. Red was clearly the royal favourite, with Princess Alexandra wearing almost exactly the same shade as the Queen, in an outfit broken only by a lacy frill which Lady Diana Spencer had already made popular. The Duchess of Gloucester (next to Princess Alexandra in the picture, opposite page, right) wore a similar deep red to set off her pink suit. The Queen's warm, chic cherry-red outfit was one of

weeks brought the five-months-long preparations for the century's most spectacular wedding to its brilliant and triumphal climax. The Queen's tour of Australasia and Sri Lanka found parallels in her son and daughter-in-law's successful visit to their Principality in October, and the news a week later that the new Princess of Wales was expecting her first baby brought an unexpected bonus to this year of celebration, and gave everyone something to look forward to in 1982.

Not that 1982 was short on incident. The quite sudden eruption of the crisis in the Falkland Islands provided the political and patriotic talking point of the year, and the Royal

her personal favourites: she had already worn it at Royal Ascot the previous year, and for her State Visit to Switzerland: it would be seen again in New Zealand in October and at Chichester as late as July 1982. By contrast, the Queen Mother opted for a quiet off-white coat and hat (above) while Princess Michael kept to the bright side

with a crisp, pure-white, close-fitting coat and small saucer-shaped hat (above, far left). These royal fashions could be seen during those few minutes when the Queen and her family came down from the Royal Box to inspect the runners from the side of the course shortly before the Derby itself. The Queen's expression gave nothing away, and she was in events right not to have betrayed too much optimism. Church Parade came fifth – a creditable showing, but one which leaves the Queen with horse-racing ambitions to fulfil.

The 1981 Derby heralded a year of almost unprecedented activity for the Royal Family. Just over a week later came the drama of the now notorious incident during the Trooping the Colour ceremonial, and the following

Family were not isolated from its consequences. From the departure of Prince Andrew in the *Invincible* at the beginning of April to the services of commemoration and charity galas in aid of the dependants of the fallen, the entire Family was in one way or another involved from start to finish.

To crown the success of the campaign, the birth of Prince William justified the national celebration. His christening on 4th August, the Queen Mother's 82nd birthday, provided an apt reminder of the continuity of monarchy, reinforced to date by Prince Harry's birth, the coming of age of several of his cousins, the Queen's 60th and the Queen Mother's 85th birthdays, and a profusion of colourful royal events at home and abroad.

occasion will be remembered, thanks to the meticulous arrangements by Lord Maclean, for going exactly according to plan, for the superb selection of music chosen by the royal couple and for the faultless timing of every element in the complex timetable of procedures. Security was necessarily strong but pleasantly unobtrusive; arrests took place in single figures only, and for deeds no more anarchic than street-trading or pickpocketing. The seventy-minute-long service, held, unlike any comparable royal wedding since 1501, in St Paul's Cathedral, crystallised everything

memorable: the fluffed lines from bride and groom, the Speaker's melodramatic reading of the Lesson, the Archbishop's short address, as cleverly designed as his new ice-blue cape and mitre, the restless fidgeting of the younger bridesmaids, the gradual relaxation in the Queen's demeanour, the occasional tear on the Queen Mother's cheek. Like all wedding days it was very much the bride's hour, and her superb puffed dress of ivory silk encrusted with a thousand sequins and mother of pearl embedded in fussy lace panels and frills, reinforced her claim to popular attention. As Lady Diana she was cheered to the echo on leaving Clarence House in the Glass Coach, and as Princess of Wales the return journey was positively deafening. The symbol and one lasting memory of the day was the now

The wedding of the Prince and Princess of Wales on 29th July 1981 outshone all previous royal events, with the possible exception of the Queen's Coronation, in terms of colour, spectacle, the acknowledgement of tradition and the depth and sincerity of popular acclaim. In a year which had seen its fair share of domestic troubles the

celebrated balcony kiss – a rare moment of royal spontaneity on a formal occasion. The official photographs were much more studied, for the most part, though Lord Lichfield captured a couple of moments of sheer fun. And balloons on the going-away carriage extended the sense of fun to the end.

The honeymoon began at Broadlands. No pictures exist save those taken privately on the last morning of the stay; some of them are on display at the mansion itself. No concession was made to the demands of publicity after the most public of courtships and the most universally witnessed of weddings. Three days of peace and serenity on English soil were all the Prince and Princess asked and, in the haven which great-uncle Mountbatten had made his own, and where his nephew the Duke of Edinburgh had taken his bride in 1947, the royal couple got it. Around them was

indeed a large part – was for the couple personally but there could be no doubt that the islanders were taking every opportunity to reaffirm their British sympathies in the face of Spanish attempts to take control of Gibraltar and the refusal of King Juan Carlos to attend the Royal Wedding in protest against this very day's proceedings. The 40-minute drive to the quayside in a borrowed Triumph Stag was an emotional experience for everyone (bottom left) and the farewells were sincere and quite moving (below, and bottom pictures). Alone at last they spent twelve days

a strong security presence: within they were with discreet friends and had the use of a 6,000-acre estate in the heart of Hampshire.
On 1st August they travelled to Eastleigh Airport to fly to Gibraltar for the beginning of the foreign leg of the honeymoon. Prince Charles piloted an Andover of the Queen's Flight, leaving his wife as a passenger in the same way that he had, it was rumoured, left her at Broadlands one morning while he went fishing for trout in the Test.
The flight lasted four hours and the royal arrival was wildly feted in a town vibrant with red white and blue. Part of the welcome –

soaking up the sun and visiting one Mediterranean island after another from the Royal Yacht *Britannia* (opposite page top). They swam and windsurfed, toured and explored until on 12th August they reached Egypt as guests of the ill-fated President Sadat. Seven weeks after they took their leave, he was dead, and Prince Charles was again in Cairo to pay his last respects.

But all were unsuspecting at Balmoral when on 19th August the Prince and Princess met the Press at the Brig O'Dee (this page). And even the Princess agreed that it was "one of the best places in the world."

One of the most tactful and well-received royal decisions of 1981 was that the Prince and Princess of Wales would begin their public life's work together with a three-day visit to Wales itself. After a prolonged holiday at Balmoral, during which the only public engagement they under-took was the traditional royal attendance at the Braemar Gathering early in September, it seemed not only desirable but also a natural consequence of

Castle (left and below far left), where Prince Charles was ceremonially invested as Prince of Wales in July 1969. Here they were met formally – and informally (below and below left) by Lord Snowdon as Constable of the Castle. After spending an hour there, they were off to Bangor and Plas

their position and title that they should choose the Principality as the venue of their first public engagements.

Their schedule was one of the sort normally associated with State visits; eleven or twelve hours each day, excluding travelling time to the first engagement and from the last. Lunch never exceeded an hour. With eighteen towns to visit it was very much a whistle-stop tour, reminiscent of Gladstone's election campaigns.

On 27th October the Prince and Princess paid visits to Deeside Leisure Centre (above) and Shotton, Rhyl and Caernarfon

Newydd, rounding off a day which surprised even the Press with its popular enthusiasm. Wind of North Wales' reception prompted the people of the south-west of the Principality to turn out in vast numbers the following day. They watched the royal couple visit St David's Cathedral (opposite page, bottom left) for a service which revealed that the Princess had not yet learned very much Welsh, and they stood in pouring rain to greet them at Haverfordwest, Carmarthen and Llandeilo. A superb gala concert at Swansea, after which the Princess was surrounded by youngsters offering gifts (bottom

left and centre), completed a hectic second day.

The final day, 29th October, brought the tour to the South where the public response was at its wildest. The day began with the opening of the Young Farmers' Club at the Royal Welsh Showground at Llanelwedd (far left) and there were subsequent walkabouts in Pontypridd (left) and Brecon (below and bottom). During a

visit to Llwynypia Hospital the Prince and Princess inspected the maternity wing and Prince Charles spoke of the benefits of fathers seeing their children born. His words hit the next day's papers, though no-one suspected the news of the Princess' own pregnancy, which was announced to a delighted nation the following week.

Since reaching 80 in December 1981, Princess Alice has often resolved to reduce her tally of engagements. But that's easier said than done: "The trouble is that when you have been associated with organisations for many years and someone pleads with you to do

something you did for them last year, or they say it's all going to be a terrible flop if you don't go, what can you do?" Her staff see it differently, marvelling as she finds excuses to do things which a less resolute octogenarian would happily dodge.

She is probably as unconvinced of her age as anyone meeting her would be. A lively mind, a deceptive sense of humour and a phenomenal memory belie her 85 years every bit as much as her impeccable deportment and the straight back which, though her figure is much more petite, recall her mother-in-law Queen Mary.

Her memory goes back to the age of two or three, but, she warned "the story is too silly to relate." She remembers her sheer terror when, while being bathed one evening, the nursery door burst open. In tumbled two elder brothers, full of mischief, and a great boot landed "with a terrible splash" into the bathtub! A more embarrassing incident

befell when she and a younger sister were to present a single bouquet of flowers – "a fatal thing to arrange" – to Princess Louise, Duchess of Argyll when she opened the Hydropathic Institution at Melrose. At the last moment her sister suddenly shouted "I don't like *her*," snatched the bouquet away and presented it to someone else. Lady Alice Montagu-Douglas-Scott's childhood was typical of

the Edwardian aristocracy: governesses, nannies and the constant shifting between her father's three residences. Her mother was reserved and, it seems, rather a distant figure: her father, Duke of Buccleuch, an MP and Lord Lieutenant, was busy, little seen by his children, and immensely authoritarian. Even in her twenties he refused her an allowance for her to go to East Africa, so she held an exhibition of her paintings and used the proceeds for the trip. They were exciting days; she took photographs of wildlife which won prizes when she got back home.

Life changed considerably after she married the Duke of Gloucester, King George V's third son, in 1935. They were quietly devoted to each other and she was warmly welcomed into the family. The King, then a very sick man, was "very kind to me," and Queen Mary used to invite her over to Marlborough House of an evening when the

Duke was away. King George VI kindly wrote to her in 1942, when the Duke was abroad, "Do let me know when you want to come and stay at Windsor."

Her public life took her to most parts of the world, but Barnwell, her country home in Northamptonshire, is her haven. "Our weekends are very precious," she says, and these pictures of her with her three grandchildren (opposite page) say it all. She still shines on duty, as (opposite page top right) at Crosby Hall, a student residence in Chelsea, on 17th March, and was thrilled at

having her 80th birthday honoured by the presentation of a new rose, Blesma Soul, to her at Kensington Palace on 6th January (this page).

Her birthday fell on Christmas Day, when the entire Royal Family was at Windsor. Did she have a party? She checked a hollow laugh: "There's *always* a party. Princess Alexandra and I shared the cake!"

(Centre left) On 19th January Princess Alexandra paid a visit to Alexandra House at Bromley in Kent, the headquarters of the Cystic Fibrosis Research Trust of which she is Patron. On 17th February (left and below left) she was escorted round the exhibition "Excavating in Egypt" which opened that day at the British Museum. The exhibition, mounted to celebrate the centenary of the Egypt Exploration Society, did not include a small section of the Sphinx's beard which the Egyptian authorities have for some time been hoping to retrieve from the British Museum's custody and restore to its rightful place on the Sphinx at the foot of the Giza pyramids.

(Opposite page) Princess Alexandra in animated mood when she attended a fashion show at the Japanese Embassy Residence in London on 25th January. The show, presented by designer Hanai Mori, was staged in aid of the Mental Health Foundation of which the Princess is Patron. She and her husband, the Hon Angus Ogilvy, were treated to a long succession of vivid and elegant designs, drawn from many different national cultures and betraying influences of fashions past and present (right).
The Princess' 1982 engagements began somewhat earlier than those of most members of the Royal Family, and January was a comparatively busy month.

Penlee is one of those names which, unknown to 99% of Britain's population for generations, suddenly becomes a household word for decades. It is to the history of the sea what Lewisham and Harrow are to the railways, Aberfan to the coal industry, Flixborough to the chemical industry. On 19th December 1981, in the grip of one of the iciest autumns for years, a coaster, the *Union Star,* listing helplessly in mountainous seas, tried in vain to reach shelter on the South Cornish coast. In an attempt to save the eight people on board, the Penlee lifeboat *Solomon Browne* set out in impossible weather and amid a confusion of signals from the distressed ship. Her mission was doomed: the lifeboat was pushed remorselessly towards the rocks where in

men to their deaths. The church, which overlooks the stricken village, had three of the dead crew buried in its churchyard, and the RNLI flag fluttered noisily at half mast as the Duke and Duchess arrived to be greeted by a guard of honour made up of 25 lifeboatmen, some of them related to the victims of the disaster. Inside were five hundred local people, crammed in as nothing before witnessed there. A further 200 people huddled together in a marquee to which the service was relayed. RNLI branches throughout Britain had requested places for representatives, but had to be told that the service was strictly limited to local interest and that room for wider public condolence would be available at a memorial service to be held at Truro

heaving seas she was smashed to pieces. Eight of her volunteer crew died, and in that one terrible venture five women were widowed and a dozen children rendered fatherless.

In the wake of the immediate tragedy, help came from all parts of the country. Even before an enquiry could get under way a voluntary fund was set up and thousands of pounds poured in to help the bereaved families and set the tiny village community back on its feet again. On 22nd January, the 81st anniversary of one death – that of Queen Victoria – which unleashed national grief of a different kind, the Duke of Kent, as President of the Royal National Lifeboat Institution, and the Duchess of Kent, attended a Family Service of Remembrance and Thanksgiving in the Parish Church in Mousehole.

It was a sharp, windswept day, but the skies were blue and little indication existed of the monstrous conditions which only a month before had sent

Cathedral the following month. The service lasted barely three quarters of an hour, and was very simple. The Duke of Kent read the lesson and a local television personality, Mr Clive Gunnell, gave an address praising selflessness and preferring the regenerative spirit to the cold stone memorial. When it was all over the Duke and Duchess, accompanied by

the Vicar, the Reverend Hugh Cadman, went to the vicarage to meet the bereaved families privately. The Duchess, clutching a wrapped bunch of flowers presented to her there, assured them that her sympathy was with them all. "I hope this is a day you will never forget, but also a day that will never come again," she said. To Mrs Mary Greenhalgh, whose husband's death had left her as licensee of the Ship Inn, the Duchess made the promise that when she was next in Cornwall on holiday she would come to her pub and have a drink. Both the Duke and the Duchess gave full rein to the only sentiment they could possibly contribute. "They were very sympathetic and expressed the hope that we would be able to pick up the threads of our lives," said one woman. The Duke was poignantly impressed. "It was a deeply moving service," he said. "It was magnificent to meet the families. They showed so much courage

and were such a great inspiration."

Since that solemn royal day the courage has continued. Funds poured in from all parts of the country and beyond its shores. A new contingent of men from Penlee and Mousehole have offered themselves as replacements for their lost neighbours in the unending and invaluable service of the RNLI. Slowly, and not without the distress which fundamental readjustment in the full glare of publicity invariably brings, life has begun to assume something approaching normality. But the personal tragedy lives on, with a severity which blights each succeeding birthday, wedding anniversary and Christmas celebration with its persistent reminder that a loved one is irretrievably absent. Only after other national and international calamities had

overwhelmed the horror of Penlee could its widows and orphans grieve privately at last. But they were touched by the memory of that royal involvement in that very hour when the need for consolation and moral support was greatest. For one afternoon this short but heartfelt royal visit brought the nation's attention to the plight of one of its smallest villages, bereft of a proportion of its manhood which in a major city would have been regarded as a national disaster. Here and now the disaster existed only within the heart of a tiny community where no-one remained unaffected by the reality of what lifeboatmen the world over regard as an occupational hazard.

On 2nd February Queen Elizabeth the Queen Mother undertook her second public engagement of 1982 when she visited Canada House to open its new Cultural Centre. After her arrival she was taken up to the High Commissioner's Office for a short private meeting. A quarter of an hour later she came down the stairs (below) escorted by the High Commissioner Mrs Jean Casselman Wadds (below right) and led by a piper – Lieutenant Mike Ward of the Royal Canadian Dragoons. Once into the auditorium at the foot of the stairs, she declared the Cultural Centre open and received a vote of thanks from the Canadian Minister of Culture and Public Affairs, Mr John Graham.

the "silver and blue train" as it was familiarly known – a 300-ton blue and aluminium CPR locomotive pulling twelve streamlined coaches over a total of more than 9,000 miles in the course of the six-week tour from Quebec to Vancouver and back to Halifax. At every station – and with a full programme which left very little time for relaxation there were many stations – there was a crowd to greet the King and Queen. Like most tours this one had its formal and informal moments. For the Queen, the laying of the foundation stone for the new Supreme Court building in Ottawa was perhaps the most memorable. She mused on the fact that she, and not the King, had been asked to lay the stone,

but concluded that the choice was appropriate as "woman's position in modern society has depended upon the growth of law." Amongst the more informal interludes was the private visit to see the famous Dionne quins who had been born in Canada six years earlier. The Queen herself was credited with miraculous powers when, despite persistent rain during a drive through Winnipeg, she instructed that the car's roof should be let down so that people could see her. Almost immediately the rain stopped! But she seemed to have enough personal magic of her own. As one commentator said, "As for the Queen she appeared and the day was won. So simple in her bearing and yet so refined, so spontaneous in every move and yet so harmonious; so radiant with feminine charm and so expressive of emotion, she also found the true words for every occasion and every person." The Queen enjoyed the tour too. "It made us," she confided to the Canadian Prime Minister Mr Mackenzie King.

The tour was almost as famous for the few days the King and Queen spent in the United States, where they were the guests of President Franklin Roosevelt and his accomplished wife Eleanor. The President's informal style was much appreciated by his guest, the modest, retiring King, and their personal letters to each other – "My dear President Roosevelt," "My dear King George" – reflected the kindred spirits. Perhaps the most informal incident of the trip came when, after a private evening dinner and a long talk, the President suddenly said to the King: "Well, young man, it's time for you to go to bed!"

Apart from the great personal success the King and Queen scored with the President, the triumphant reception accorded to them by the people of New York and the Atlantic seaboard surpassed all precedents. George III's descendant and his wife conquered the old colonies at the first attempt!

None of the Queen Mother's subsequent visits to Canada ever equalled the scale and sparkle of the 1939 tour. But in 1954 she was back again, spending five days in Ottawa. Because of her visit she was unable to be in

The ceremony was short but it kept alive the Queen Mother's links with Canada which were forged almost forty-three years before. In 1939, less than three years after their accession, she accompanied King George VI on an exhausting and comprehensive 6-week State Visit there, which took them from coast to coast, and eclipsed even the brilliant State Visit to France the previous year. It was nearly written off when their ship *Empress of Australia* almost hit an iceberg at about the spot where *HMS Titanic* foundered in 1912, and almost on the anniversary of the tragedy. But the royal arrival at Quebec on 17th May 1939 made King George VI the first reigning British sovereign to tread on the soil of what was then fondly known as British North America. The tour was a resounding success. Travel was mostly by

London for Prince Charles' sixth birthday, but he was thrilled to receive a transatlantic telephone call from her instead. In June 1962 she went to Montreal to attend the centenary celebrations of the Black Watch (Royal Highland Regiment) of Canada, of which she is Colonel-in-Chief, and three years later celebrated the jubilee of the Toronto Scottish Regiment.

A slightly more prolonged visit was arranged in July 1967 when a 10-day programme took her to

the Atlantic provinces of New Brunswick, Nova Scotia, Prince Edward Island and Newfoundland. In June 1974 she was back again to present new Colours to each of her two regiments in Toronto and Montreal. Three years ago she paid a seven day visit to Halifax and Toronto and in July 1981 attended the bicentennial celebrations of Niagara on the Lake during another 7-day visit to Ontario. And in 1985 she was back again, proclaiming that her affection for Canada and Canadians had not diminished over the years. Her eight visits to Canada as Queen Mother and the Canadian connections she nurtures in Britain have maintained the commitment engendered by that first great tour when she herself said, "When I'm in Canada, I am a Canadian."

Prince Philip became President of World Wildlife Fund International in May 1981 and in February 1982 began one of what may become a series of crash courses to familiarise himself with conservation problems in all parts of the world. In a three-week tour

which he was serenaded (bottom right) during lunch by a local violinist.

(Below) In New Delhi Prince Philip presented the keys of two jeeps to the Asian Elephant Group at the Maurya Sheraton Hotel, after he had watched two audio visual shows detailing some of the World Wildlife Fund's Indian operations. Earlier that day he met the Prime Minister, Mrs Indira Gandhi (opposite page) and had lunch with her.

Prince Philip's 36-hour visit to Oman, where he was the guest of the Sultan (who paid a State Visit to Britain the following month) was arranged primarily to enable him to see the progress of one of the most exciting of all World Wildlife

which began on 17th February and took him to countries as far apart as Spain and Sri Lanka, he witnessed a wide range of activities from the minting of commemorative medals in Vienna to the reintroduction of captive oryx into the deserts of Oman.

In Austria he visited a compound (top right) at Haringsee where wild birds, including this ferocious-looking bearded vulture (opposite page top), are reared for research purposes, and a bird sanctuary (above right) at Marchegg, near the Czechoslovakian border. He had earlier been taken on a waggon ride round the Seewinkel to tour extensive wetlands populated with geese and other marsh birds, after

Fund's hundreds of projects. A decade ago the Arabian white oryx was almost extinct in the wild, a victim, like so many other species, of the trade in horn. The last few were rounded up and reared in a long-term programme of captivity and have only just been released back into the wild. The Duke arrived at the desert base at Yalooni, a two-hour helicopter journey from Muscat, to see how the oryx's reintroduction was progressing.

On arrival he met Dr and Mrs Mark Stanley-Price who run the project (bottom left) and was taken by landrover to where the oryx could be seen.

Unfortunately the previous night had brought a 1½″ rainfall, the first rain for 5 years, and some of the Duke's wanderings on foot became a little hazardous (left). But he was able to see ten pure white oryx grazing placidly among acacia, eronbergiana and prosopis trees, and the project staff were particularly proud that one of the oryx had produced a healthy calf, now nine months old, which was adapting as well as the adults to its new environment. The Duke was fascinated to meet the local Bedou tribesmen (far left) who, armed with rifles, now have the job of protecting the herd from poachers.

On 7th March Prince Philip's tour took him to Port Sudan where the Sudanese Navy was

waiting to take him and World Wildlife Fund officials to a coral reef some twenty miles out to sea. The expedition had the advantage of the best weather of the tour, though the swell during the outward journey kept a few of the passengers fairly subdued. Even the Duke was on the point of succumbing towards the end, and on disembarking opted to climb the lighthouse *before* taking lunch! From the top of the lighthouse – "257 steps, if you're interested," he said on the way down – the brilliant variations in the sea's colour could be seen, while a walk along the jetty brought the sight

During his two-day visit to India, Prince Philip travelled from Jaipur to visit a tiger reserve at Sariska, about 150 miles south of New Delhi. On his arrival at the reserve headquarters tea was served in the garden and the layout of the reserve was explained (opposite page, bottom right) with details of the forty or so species of animals and birds which are known to inhabit it. A three-jeep convoy then left (centre pictures) for a fascinating two-hour journey deep into the reserve. There was

no risk of being met by tigers, which come out only at night, but a large variety of wildlife was in evidence. Deer, neatly camouflaged in the dense woodland, were betrayed by shafts of sunlight filtering through, but showed little sign of nervousness as the jeeps slowed to allow their passengers a glimpse. The occasional jackal was spotted, blue-bull and rhesus monkeys abounded, the nests of weaver-birds dangled and swung from tall trees, and buzzards drifted high against

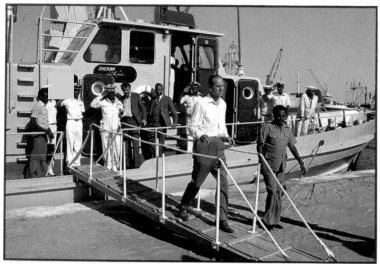

of brightly coloured fish, crabs and shoals of sardinellos in the rocky shallows (right). Prince Philip was taken by boat to look for fish in the deeper waters (above right) before returning to Port Sudan (centre and top left). From there he went to Suakin – almost a ghost town now since it literally fell to pieces thirty years ago or so – to record his visit to a small research centre (opposite page, bottom left).

lofty crags. On the way back the Duke stopped at a look-out post from which tourists (who were not admitted on this day) can watch for tigers – but although that part of the visit was extended into the early hours of dusk, no tiger was sighted. On the return journey the stench of rotting meat heralded the quite gripping spectacle of a score of buzzards tearing at the corpse of some unfortunate animal, and flaunting grisly morsels of dripping flesh in savage beaks. For this is no animal sanctuary,

is a problem the Germans will have to sort out for themselves. I am sure you can find a compromise on this."

He went to Sri Lanka to see the operation of a massive project which involves the reorganisation of whole communities of elephants with human populations and industrial complexes to provide the most efficient interplay between the multiple needs of each. He visited Sri Lanka's two biggest sanctuaries – at Yale and Wilpattu – and during a visit to

into the Parque Donana, a huge – indeed Europe's largest – wetland wildlife preserve, where he spent most of the afternoon and evening being driven from habitat to habitat.

In Madrid there was a meeting with his cousin King Juan Carlos of Spain; and the affectionate welcome given to him by Queen Sophie made it obvious that despite the fracas over the Royal Wedding, the personal relationships between the English and Spanish royal families were as strong as ever.

except in that it is protected from the ravages of man. The cruelties of nature – as man might see it – are allowed their course in the interests of the delicate balance of life in the wild, and the fact was uncompromisingly illustrated by this chance encounter with the stark reality.

The Duke's tour also took him to Egypt, where poor weather unfortunately put paid to a visit to an oasis in the Sinai and

limited his activities to a view of the Giza Pyramids and, as he somewhat bitterly put it, "a look at Cairo's traffic."

An earlier leg of the tour found the Duke in the midst of a controversy in the province of Schleswig-Holstein, in northern Germany. Here the government is proposing to build a six-mile dyke across a nature reserve of 8400 acres, and ecologists are convinced that the project will threaten the natural uses to which this marshland is put. Hundreds of thousands of migratory birds use it, millions of sea birds find it a convenient breeding ground, and it also houses shallow-living sea life like crabs and mussels.

The Duke had to tread gingerly between the interests of the administration, who were concerned to prevent the loss of life and property in the event of a severe flood, and the ecologists who feared the loss of wildlife amenities. He achieved his neutral stance with his usual accomplishment. Speaking in fluent German he said, "Both interests are perfectly valid. This

a zoo in Colombo, he was presented with a baby elephant, named Geetha, which is now in London Zoo.

He visited further projects in Italy and Tunisia and finished the entire tour with a 2-day visit to Spain. Here he visited the Gonzales Byass sherry bodegas before joining a field trip at Sanlucar de Barrameda near Jerez. He enjoyed an open air lunch before crossing the Rio Guadalquivir by navy launch

Prince Philip returned to Heathrow airport on 12th March at the end of his three week tour, during which it was announced that he had been appointed Vice-President of the International Union for the Conservation of Nature and Natural Resources – the scientific branch of the World Wildlife Fund.

One of the most prestigious diplomatic events of February was the Ambassadorial Ball Soirée Française held on 22nd February at Grosvenor House in aid of the United Nations Association and UNICEF. This year's royal guest was the Duchess of Gloucester, sparkling as always in appearance and in form, seen (above and opposite page) as she arrived for the Soirée. The distinguished company included the patrons of honour – twenty five Ambassadors and High Commissioners – and another 25 patrons representing a vast range of national life – Margaret Duchess of Argyll and Lulu, Group-Captain Leonard Cheshire and Stirling Moss, Yehudi Menuhin and Esther Rantzen. Eric Morecambe, another patron, was there and the Duchess clearly enjoyed his company (top pictures). So much so that she may even have been tempted to appear in his next show!

The programme for the six-hour entertainment was superb. After the champagne reception, the guests were serenaded during a dinner of cream of cress soup, seafood pancake, suprême de volaille and cherries with praline ice cream. A fashion spectacular by the New Bond Street fashion house Ungaro followed, before Johnny Howard and his Orchestra led the dancing until the midnight cabaret. A couple of raffles were held, with holidays in Bali, India and Tunisia as prizes in one, and jewellery, clothes and wines contributing to a 13-part prize

list in the other. For those with energy to spare there was a discotheque until 2.00 in the morning.
The Duchess left somewhat earlier than that but even so was probably relieved that she had no engagements to fulfil the following day.

When Princess Anne married Captain Mark Phillips in November 1973 he took her, after their enviable South American honeymoon, to his married quarters, Oak Grove House, at the Royal Military Academy Sandhurst. They didn't stay there long, moving into Gatcombe Park in 1977 just

before Mark left the Army. As Colonel-in-Chief of three regiments it was probably only a matter of time before she was invited back to her husband's old stamping ground and she did indeed accept an invitation to inspect the passing-out parade of Academy graduates on 12th March.

The parade was a comparatively small one, only 89 student officers taking part. They had just graduated from Direct Course No 19, after a twenty-

week training which began in October 1981 and ended with today's confirmed commissions. The ceremonial which surrounded the royal inspection was predictable in character, highly musical and spectacularly enjoyable. A succession of musical marches accompanied the March-on Parade of Amiens and Ypres Companies, before the approach of Princess Anne and her arrival at the reviewing dais to the strains of the National Anthem. During her inspection (far left and centre left) she drew a smile from one bandsman, Sergeant Major Gordon Saunders, whom she recognised as having played for her when she lived at Sandhurst (top left). She returned to the dais for the March Past (bottom pictures) – a lengthy business involving seven changes of music, during which she found time for chirpy conversation with Colonel J E M Hughes, the College Commander of Victory College (opposite page). Princess Anne made a short closing address (opposite page bottom right) remembering her days at Sandhurst with affection, and presented the Commander's Medal to 2nd Lieutenant Andrew Gregory, the best of his course.

One newspaper called it the "laughing-out" parade. It was good to see Princess Anne, whose relationships with the Press are not always cordial, thoroughly enjoying herself for all to see.

Central London came tolerantly to a halt on the morning of 16th March as final preparations were completed for the first State Visit to Britain of His Majesty Sultan Qaboos bin Said Al Said of Oman. Persistent heavy rain in the early morning yielded before his arrival, but overcast skies made it certain that the processions from Victoria Station would be in closed carriages, as happened for the State Visit of the Nigerian President a year previously. Detachments of Household Cavalry (below) and massed

bands (left) paraded from barracks to route positions in capes and greatcoats, only the Kings Troop, Royal Horse Artillery (bottom left) sporting their resplendent gold braided uniforms as they rode towards Hyde Park to give the customary gun salutes.

The Sultan suffered his own experience of the British weather when his VC10 aircraft, preparing to land at Gatwick, was struck on the nose cone by what was described as a severe bolt of lightning, which jolted the plane's passengers but otherwise did no harm. "I've heard of 21-gun salutes," said the pilot, Denis Lowry, "but that was ridiculous." None the worse for his shock, the Sultan was greeted at Gatwick by the Duke of Gloucester and calmly emerged from the aircraft to join the Royal Train for Victoria. For many State Visitors to Britain, this habitual welcoming protocol is strange and novel,

but the Sultan would have understood it better than most. He has been a regular visitor – on semi-official as well as on several private occasions – to the country towards which he feels great affection. It was to Britain that he was sent at the age of 18 in 1958 to study privately in Suffolk before going to Sandhurst in 1960 and joining the 1st Battalion, the Cameronians, with BAOR in West Germany in 1962. It was with the aid of British officers that he overthrew his severely feudal father in 1970, after spending years in prison in Dhofar province, and the British came to his assistance three years later to put down an insurrection there, inspired by his Marxist neighbours in South Yemen (formerly British Aden). Sultan Qaboos, who owns a country house in Berkshire, loves Britain and has immense admiration and respect for the Royal Family.

His welcoming by the Queen and Prince Philip at Victoria Station (this page) was as much a personal greeting as a significant gesture in the history of the relations between Britain and Oman. As a token of his personal regard for the Queen, the Sultan had brought with him

Engineering of Clydebank disclosed a £50 million order for gas turbines for Oman's new power station. For Prince Philip (left) the welcoming ceremonies at Victoria Station carried an even more personal element, since less than a month previously he had been the Sultan's guest during his short trip to Oman as President of the World Wildlife Fund.

Other members of the Royal

an 18ct gold insignia, studded with diamonds and rubies, which the makers, Spink and Sons of London, ventured to think was probably the richest of its kind anywhere in the world. As a token of the more practical faith which the Sultan has in British technology, his visit coincided with the

announcement that he had concluded a £215 million contract with Cementation International to build a University in Oman, with the possible benefit of ancillary equipment and services worth £140 million to be provided by British firms, and before the end of the visit, John Brown

Family were also there to greet the Sultan – amongst them Princess Anne and Captain Mark Phillips (overleaf with the Duchess of Gloucester) and the Duke and Duchess of Kent (bottom right). There was a slight hitch in the welcoming ceremonies when it was discovered that Baroness Phillips, the Lord Lieutenant of London – who was supposed to introduce the Sultan to the Prime Minister – had not arrived. Apparently her newly-employed chaffeur failed to collect her from home. But protocol notwithstanding, the

Prime Minister, along with her Cabinet colleagues Foreign Secretary Lord Carrington and Home Secretary Mr William Whitelaw (below right), were duly introduced. They met again the following day at Downing Street, where Mrs Thatcher entertained the Sultan to lunch, and had "extremely friendly and cordial talks."

The journey from Victoria Station, preceded by the Sultan's inspection of the Guard of Honour, was not without incident. Just as the Queen and her guest, with Prince Philip, were leaving in the Irish State Coach, a brown Renault 16 was spotted parked in the Mall between Clarence House and Buckingham Palace. Suspecting the worst, police quickly flashed a message to the procession organisers to detour through Birdcage Walk while the car was detonated by a small controlled

The Sultan's afternoon programme followed the usual pattern – an address of welcome by the Lord Mayor of Westminster at St. James's Palace, a courtesy visit to the Queen Mother at Clarence House, and a visit to Westminster Abbey to lay a wreath on the grave of the Unknown Warrior. That evening the Queen gave a State Banquet at Buckingham Palace which the whole of the Royal Family, save Prince Andrew, Prince Edward, Princess Alice and Princess Alexandra and her husband, attended. In her speech the Queen admitted that Britain had

explosion – which revealed that it was harmless. Its owner, Michael Waterfield of Canterbury, had parked it there without realising what concern it would cause, and he later commemorated the fact by insisting that the dent in his boot, caused by the detonation, should not be knocked out. Meanwhile, however, thousands of people, many Omanis included, who had waited in the Mall for a glimpse of the royal visitor, were disappointed.

been criticised for losing interest in the Arabian peninsula but promised that "we shall keep faith with Oman."

After visiting the Prime Minister the following day, Sultan Qaboos was guest of honour at the Lord Mayor's luncheon at the Guildhall, at which the Duke of Kent was present. It was here that the Sultan made his most overtly political speech of the entire visit, condemning "Soviet imperialist interference in the Arab World" which "exploits the situation for its own ends." He urged a peaceful solution to the Palestinian problem on the basis of an honourable settlement of the plight of the Palestinians "in the interests of justice and common humanity" and was "convinced that our friends in the West have an important responsibility...in solving the problems that confront the Middle East today."

Considering how vulnerable Oman is in an area of seething international politics and vital commercial importance to the world economy, his words were both implacable against potential enemies and logically attractive towards friends. For in addition to the mainland of Oman, the Sultan rules a small triangle of land just to the north

east of the United Arab Emirates, which controls the Straits of Hormuz through which every oil tanker must pass from the Persian Gulf. He confidently promised his Guildhall hosts that all the Western World's oil which sails through the Straits to keep their economies alive, would continue to do so, and paid tribute to the contribution that Britain had made towards bringing Oman out of the backward state in which he had inherited it in

1970. In those days there was hardly a metalled road in the whole country. Now it fairly bristles with beautifully tarmac'd desert roads, airports, schools, clinics, factories, electricity systems and television. And in the forces, the process of Omanisation – the gradual handover of knowhow and leadership from the invited British forces to the Omanis – has taken its first tentative steps. The last full day of the Sultan's visit was taken up by a visit to

Bovington Camp in Dorset to see a display of British military hardware in action. The Royal Armoured Corps put on a superlative demonstration of tanks and artillery, sufficiently impressing the Sultan for him to order £35 million of Chieftain tanks for use in his own national army. On his return to London, he returned the Queen's hospitality by giving a State Banquet for her and other members of the Royal Family at Claridges. Fewer members of her family attended than at the Buckingham Palace Banquet two days before, but Princess Margaret (top and opposite

page left) and the Duchess of Gloucester (right) enhanced the occasion with their richly coloured evening gowns and sparkling jewellery. As did the Queen, who was delighted to be welcomed personally by the Sultan in this colourful finale to a most satisfactory visit.

The British Royal Family's amicable personal relations with Oman's Sultan has parallels with other tribal or hereditary rulers. Perhaps the best example is the Nepalese monarchy whose

present head King Birendra is a close personal friend of Prince Charles. The Prince, with his great-uncle Lord Mountbatten attended the King's coronation at Katmandu in 1975, and visited the King during his solo tour in December 1980. The Duke and Duchess of Gloucester spent a fortnight or so in Nepal in February 1982, and the Queen and Duke of Edinburgh paid their second

State Visit to the mountain kingdom, on their way to Australia and New Zealand early in 1986 – almost exactly a quarter of a century after their first visit there as part of a six-week tour of the East in 1961.

Over a century and a half ago Britain negotiated the Peace of Nanking with Imperial China after a comparatively brief skirmish over the opium trade. The terms were favourable to Britain: reparations of £5¾ million, the opening of five Chinese ports to British trade, and the cession of Hong Kong. Immediately, the Royal Navy recruited Hong Kong sailors into her ships and once in Britain many of them eventually settled in the great bustling, north-western port of Liverpool. The descendants of some of those Chinese recruits were presented on 2nd April 1982 to the Prince and Princess of Wales, who arrived in their maroon Rolls-Royce to perform the official opening of the Pagoda of the Hundred Harmonies on the outskirts of the City's Chinese quarter. It isn't really a pagoda at all, but its design imitates the style as closely as the purpose of the building allows. And the purpose is, quite simply, a community centre, specifically for the oldest Chinese community of its kind in Western Europe, and the second largest, next to London's Soho, in Britain. The Merseyside Chinese thus became the first in Europe to have their very own community building. So the day was one of special pride for them.

There is no getting away from the fact that Merseyside's social history this century has been a tough one. Its communities have been stricken with some of the worst effects of unemployment and poverty when times have been bad, and popular impatience with Central Government has boiled over into violence and disorder: the "Scuffers" strike of 1920, the Depression of the 1920's and 1930's, a whole series of debilitating dock strikes, and more recently the street riots in Toxteth, born, it was thought, out of racial tension and bitterness. But today the mood had changed and the thousands present were out to have a good

before," pulled her towards him and planted a decisive kiss on her cheek, momentarily giving her quite a shock. For her part the Princess made three-year-old Colin Griffiths' day when he slipped between the legs of Special Branch police officers and ran towards her to present his 70p worth of yellow tulips. He turned back towards his mother, then changed his mind and made for the Princess, said "I love you" and smothered her with kisses. As she bent down to hug him, the crowd cheered them both on, thrilled by the spontaneity of it all. "I'm not

day.

Everyone seemed to enter into the spirit of elation, including the Prince and Princess, who were at their most delightfully informal. Prince Charles watched as his wife received a long line of VIPs in the welcoming ceremony, and decided to join the back of the queue. When his turn came he said, "I believe we've met

really surprised at what he did," said his mother afterwards. "He really adores her. She's his favourite person and he loves to watch her on television."

The opening ceremony was typically spectacular. The Prince and Princess each painted-in the eyes of the hundredweight-and-a-half ceramic dragon at the entrance to the building in the

manner of the New Year festivities, when the dragon comes to life. The pagoda's dragon in fact had electric light bulbs for eyes, giving the building a glowing identity at night.

The royal couple toured the centre and saw the Chinese inscription on the outer wall reading: "This community will strive for prosperity, harmony and the aspiration for future multi-racial integration and understanding with all peoples." Remembering Toxteth, they were noble sentiments.

The centre itself realised an aspiration – that of Mr Brian Tai-Sheng Wang, who at only 32 is a full-time Community Liaison Officer and who in the seven years since he arrived from Taiwan has devoted his time to creating the circumstances in which young Chinese might obtain educational and career opportunities. His efforts have placed him in high regard: he did much to secure the £¼ million needed for the centre – £228,000 from the Inner City Partnership, the remainder from local fund-raising events.

The Prince and Princess were entertained to an eight-course lunch prepared by cooks from two of Liverpool's Chinese restaurants. It lived up to the reputation of all Chinese meals: there were spare ribs, crispy stuffed phoenix-tail prawns with spring onions, fried duckling with jasmin, sweet and sour fish, chicken in yellow bean sauce and platters of fruits offered by what were mysteriously referred to as "celestial ladies." Over lunch, and during the folk dancing display that accompanied it, the Princess spoke to Mr Wang's 30-year-old wife Nora. As luck would have it she too was expecting a baby – a month earlier than the Princess – so there was plenty to talk about. But Mrs Wang remained inscrutable afterwards: "We talked quite a lot about the sort of thing that ladies like us do talk about." So evidently did Prince Charles. He told Mrs Christine Cheetham and Mrs Jill Walker, both also pregnant: "It must be something in the water." Surely he must know better than that!

On 13th April, the Tuesday after Easter, Queen Elizabeth the Queen Mother left Clarence House for the Royal Albert Hall to attend a gala concert which, according to an understatement in the programme notes,

Philharmonic Orchestra, with whom he was to sing, and the Queen Mother's presence as Patron of the Orchestra at a concert staged as part of its National Appeal made the evening one of superlatives.

promised "to be one of London's musical events of the year." It was in fact the only scheduled appearance at a concert in the United Kingdom in 1982 of that superlative tenor opera singer Luciano Pavarotti. The occasion was all the more special because Pavarotti himself had substantially reduced his fees to help the Royal

Indeed, when a recording of the concert was shown on television a few days later, it was on the cards that opera had recruited a substantial number of new admirers.

At 47, Pavarotti had acquired every tribute the opera world could possibly heap on one man. For a singer whose professional début did not occur until the age of 26, it must be praise indeed to be commended for having a voice which in various ways can be likened to Caruso's, Gigli's or Björling's. He first performed in England in 1962 – at Covent Garden, which occupies a very important place in the milestone history of his career.

The programme was by modern standards a colossal one, with four orchestral pieces and seven operatic arias including three by Verdi and two by Puccini, and after the concert Pavarotti was introduced to the Queen Mother (above left). Opera is not thought to be the Queen Mother's listening forte though she has had an accomplished ear for music since childhood, and when young sang "very prettily," according to her music mistress. But it is inconceivable that Pavarotti's performance did less than rivet her – these pictures show her looking as fresh as a daisy, lively and with that famous wagging finger (opposite page bottom left) in animated conversation with the celebrity whose singing she unreservedly enjoyed. For a great-grandmother striding confidently towards her 82nd birthday, she looked a picture of appreciation, was charmed by Pavarotti's chivalrous gestures – reminiscent of some Renaissance

established and she may have passed a few tips on.
Financially the concert was a massive success, and the Royal Philharmonic will have been pleased and thankful for that. The box office takings showed the largest amount their performances had ever drawn at any concert hall anywhere in the

world – almost £150,000. For an organisation which at some of its concerts pays back to the Government in VAT more than it receives in grants, that must be compensation enough, but it was also satisfying to know that this was not an occasion solely for the wealthy. Of the 6,000 tickets sold, 3,500 were available at £15 or less, including 1,000 student tickets at only £2.50 each. The result was the largest "live" audience ever to hear Pavarotti in the UK, and every one of them, like the Queen Mother, surely satisfied with the exquisite performance of a man who according to the title of one of his own records is "King of the High C's."

gallant (far right), and as thrilled as Pavarotti was honoured by the presentation to her of one of his eight records currently available (above right). And did they, perhaps for a few brief moments, exchange the latest gossip on the equestrian scene? Pavarotti's interest in horse racing and thoroughbred breeding is as recent as the Queen Mother's is well

The thirty-first Badminton Three-day Event – it has been held every year since its inauguration in 1949 – got underway in the grounds of the late Duke of Beaufort's Gloucestershire mansion on 15th April. This prestigious, well-attended and thorough test of all-round horsemanship, with the Whitbread Trophy and a prize of £3,000 for the winner, attracted a gate of almost 200,000 people, and a field of seventy-nine competitors. Among them were twenty initiates aged less than 25, as well as the much more seasoned campaigners, Princess Anne (below) and her husband Captain Mark Phillips (right).

sadly, he ultimately attended only as a spectator.

The dressage took up two days of the Badminton programme, and both Princess Anne (No 72) and Captain Phillips (No 83) competed on the second day. Both had submitted their horses to the usual veterinary inspection on the evening of the 14th April, and each horse was declared sound. But despite this and the previous day's practice runs (below and right), Captain Phillips' mount Classic Lines conceded 60.6 dressage penalty points and left him down the field. Princess Anne, who had not competed at Badminton since 1979, fared rather better with a

Princess Anne (seen above riding the Queen's horse Stevie B in the first phase of the competition, the dressage, on 16th April) has never yet won at Badminton, but Captain Phillips, like Lucinda Prior-Palmer-Green who won in 1973, 1976, 1977 and 1979, has run out victor on a record four different occasions – in 1971 and 1972 on

his horse Great Ovation, in 1974 on the Queen's horse Columbus, and in 1981 on Lincoln, a horse sponsored by Range Rover Team, as part of the deal he made with Land Rover Ltd in 1980. The sponsorship, arranged amid fierce public criticism, brought Captain Phillips more than £75,000 in two years, including over £10,000 in prize

money – mostly from his tally of sixteen victories in 1981. Shortly before Badminton it was announced that the sponsoring partnership would be continued until December 1983, with an option to extend for two further years. This took Captain Phillips into the reckoning for the 1984 Olympics at Los Angeles, an event at which,

final total of 58.2 penalties. The following day, fortunes were quite dramatically reversed. Captain Phillips, who later declared that he was "thrilled with Classic Lines' performance in the dressage and cross-country," came home with a clear round in the cross country phase – recognised as one of the most gruelling of its kind in

Europe, with its total of 32 obstacles comprising steps, ditches, hedges, rails, fences, ski-jumps and lakes. This performance lifted him to eventual 14th place, two places short of the entitlement to the smallest prize of £125. Princess Anne did not, however, have such a good day. She had already had one of her regular altercations with the army of photographers who have followed her equestrian career with unstinting interest, when her exasperation reached breaking point the previous day. "Why don't you all grow up," she told them. "You've been taking the same pictures of me every day for three days. Why

don't you naff off. Go on, shove off." In no mood to do either, the photographers were waiting for her at the eighteenth fence in the cross country – the upturned punt barring entry into the lake. This is usually the spot where her husband comes a cropper, but this time Stevie B's hooves clipped the punt and Princess

for them both. In June 1981 Mark had been in the winning British team at the European championships at Hooge Mierde in Holland and was joined by Princess Anne at the Burghley Horse Trials in September – she won there in 1971 to take the European Championship that year. Unfortunately both of them landed in water ditches during the cross country, and came away unplaced.

October was another bad month: although Captain Phillips won £1,500 prize money at Wylye Horse Trials near Salisbury, Princess Anne was nearly knocked down by another rider when she was helping to rebuild one of the fallen fences. Later that month Mark went to

Anne, unable to control his imbalance, nosedived with him into the lake (opposite page). She retrieved the horse and paddled out of the lake, her white nylon breeches transparent and her riding boots full of water. Surprisingly cheerful – or at least philosophical (top right) – she decided to retire from the event and trotted off back to the stables, though not before she had cast a final malediction the way of the photographers. "I hope you're all happy. You've got what you wanted now."

So ended the Phillipses twelfth Badminton challenge, in what had been a busy equestrian year compete in Australia, where he found considerably more interest being shown in the rumours of a rift in his marriage. In a radio interview, for which he was said to have asked a fee of £6,000, he faced up to the long-running stories of a liaison between him and former BBC newsreader Angela Rippon, who had been commissioned to write a book called "Mark Phillips, The Man and His Horses" – which, incidentally she launched at Badminton on 15th April. He denied any romance, saying that he and Princess Anne had got to know Miss Rippon very well – "after all, it takes a long time to write a book. Princess Anne and

I are not at all happy about the rumours. Nor was Miss Rippon – she too is happily married." The same month brought an astonishing statement from Councillor Jim Spencer, a Liberal member of Otley Town Council in West Yorkshire who, in a debate about the local horse-riding fraternity, protested that "horses are ridden by base and coarse people like Princess Anne." Just a joke, he said afterwards.
Captain Phillips' luck failed to improve over the New Year. He had to admit that he needed a complete break from horses after a heavy 18-month

schedule. He had taken an enforced rest when his back began to play up in November, and decided to prolong it over Christmas. He then found himself a stone and a half overweight as his training deadline approached and had to work hard to get himself in trim again.
In January he was unable to get from Gatcombe to Upminster where he was due to compete in the Martell Cognac Championships; heavy snow delayed his train from Stroud, and attempts to charter a helicopter failed. By February he was campaigning to save Aintree, now in one of its recurring death throes; he had jumped the course back in 1979 and thought it "one of the greatest experiences of my life: it would be a tragic loss."
March saw both him and Princess Anne back in the saddle with a vengeance: at Crookham Horse Trials he rode his "second" horse Blizzard II,

while she competed on her younger horse Soul Song. They both competed later at Downlands Horse Trials near Liphook, and Mark was out again at Wendover Horse Trials towards the end of the month. And, as a postscript to Badminton, Princess Anne rode Soul Song at Hagley Horse Trials in Worcestershire in April. He refused at the water ditch, and she fell in. Plus ça change…
Princess Anne has long been branded the black sheep of the Royal Family, and often without the tolerant endearments which that expression often connotes.

Her frequent brushes with the Press – usually at some equestrian event – and the Press' own retaliatory sarcasm against her whenever she uses the word "one" to mean "I" or "me," has brought the Princess' public image into what at one stage looked like irretrievable disfavour.

One accusation frequently levelled against her is that she unnecessarily distances herself from the Press and her public. Yet she is the best known of all the Queen's children in the sense that she has invited a considerable amount of publicity into her activities both public and private. Ever since the

rather disastrous pre-wedding interview she and Captain Phillips gave in November 1973 for transmission by both television corporations – "It was a night to turn monarchists into republicans and republicans into monarchists," said one critic – interviews and filming facilities have been given regularly in and around Oak Grove House at Sandhurst, and Gatcombe Park. As a result, we have enjoyed in particular a unique insight into the way the Princess and her husband throw themselves into their consuming equestrian pastimes.

Until the '80s, Princess Anne rarely spoke of her public life – how she approaches it, how important she feels it is, what she gets out of it. That was partly remedied when she was interviewed in December 1981 for the ITV programme "Princess Anne, Her Working Life." In it she envisaged that her

kindred spirit in 10-year-old Alexander Lochore, whose father is a friend of Princess Anne, he began racing round the collecting ring, squealing and shouting as he darted between his mother's legs, swinging round them and throwing both parents off balance with some pretty physical charges. Captain

Phillips remonstrated (opposite page right), so did Princess Anne, but Peter was in too boisterous a mood to take the hint. Eventually, Princess Anne took him off (above) to one of her grooms and he was led, protesting, out of the compound.

children would be free to pursue their careers without having to perform official duties. She cited Princess Margaret's children as examples, but she might more aptly have chosen the family of her great-aunt, the late Princess Royal. Her brothers produced families who answered the royal call, but her own sons, Lord Harewood and Mr Gerald Lascelles, are conveniently off the royal hook.

As if to demonstrate that he has no intention of being very royal, Princess Anne's son Peter ran amok at Badminton, giving the crowds more entertainment than they had paid to see. Finding a

Two of the most recent royal regulars at Badminton are Prince Michael and Princess Michael of Kent, seen here on 17th April enjoying the thrills and spills of the cross country Speed and Endurance Test, as well as a few much more personal moments (bottom picture and opposite page extreme right). Their attendance each year (including 1981, only days before the Princess gave birth to her second child) is no mere social appearance. Both share wide equestrian interests. Prince Michael often goes hunting, though not always with satisfactory results: in October 1981 he was one of a succession of riders who were thrown from their horses at a Meet of the Quorn in Leicestershire. Princess Michael, a keen huntswoman too, supports equestrian events close to her home at Nether Lyppiatt, competes in horse trials and point-to-points, and is rated highly enough to have made the front page of *Horse and Hound*.

1982. Starring Jeremy Irons, it was one of three official British entries that year and Prince Michael backed it financially. Among the films and plays Prince and Princess Michael saw in the same year were "The Little Foxes" in March, when they met Elizabeth Taylor; the charity premiere of

to the Solent for Cowes Week, and took both him and his wife to Rhode Island in 1983 to support the British entry *Victory* in the America's Cup. At the other extreme of their combined interests is their penchant for the arts. Like her talented mother-in-law, Princess Marina, Princess Michael paints, though "very badly" she admits, "in water colours," preferring to

The horse world forms only part of the royal couple's sporting interests. Despite the accident sixteen years ago which almost killed him, Prince Michael has never lost his enthusiasm for bobsleighing. As President of the British Bobsleigh Association he agreed to open the Thorpe Training Run for bobsleigh practice in Chertsey in September 1981, and the following January visited the British team at St Moritz as they trained for their annual assault on the World Championships. Prince Michael's interest in sailing takes him frequently

paint still lifes and flowers: "I don't paint as well as Princess Marina did and feel I have a lot to live up to." Her ambition is to have one of her works accepted by the Society of Women Artists, whose annual exhibition she opened at the Mall Galleries in February.

The cinema and theatre have Prince Michael's support: he visited the Cannes Film Festival to follow the fortunes of the film "Moonlighting" in May

"On Golden Pond" at the Empire Leicester Square, and the new £1½ million production of "The Pirates of Penzance" at the Savoy.

Rumour had it that the Prince and Princess could even be going into television, with Prince Michael as non-executive director of the television company AMTV and his wife as a breakfast television presenter. But it proved a false hope: he is kept busy enough with

his interests in the City; she has probably had her fill of the media, and has anyway been trying for five years to finish her book on Elizabeth of Bohemia – the Winter Queen, daughter of our own King James I and a direct ancestress of the House of Windsor.

It was during a visit to Holland to research the book that, in February 1982, the Princess was taken ill with severe abdominal pains. She was rushed off to King Edward VII Hospital for Officers in Marylebone, where two days of

catch up on her work. And work, which over the years has taken her and Prince Michael from their London residence, Kensington Palace, to as far afield as Belize, to represent the Queen at independence in 1981, seems to be colourful, varied, interesting and enjoyable. Certainly few have taken up the royal role with as much unashamed gusto as has Princess Michael, with her regal bearing, superbly chosen wardrobe, glittering jewels and expansive gestures. David Bailey's official photograph of

examination and tests amid rumours that she was pregnant or had suffered a miscarriage, showed that her gall bladder was the cause of the trouble. Prince Michael was at her bedside for most of this worrying time, and even brought their two children to see their mother who "was missing them, and the doctors thought it would be a tonic for her." Lord Frederick looked a picture in his piped jacket and knickerbockers. After an operation for the removal of her gall bladder, Princess Michael emerged from hospital "feeling fine" on 1st March, and went back to Kensington Palace to

her in a rich blue gown with extravagant ruffles and puffed sleeves was a classic of royal portraiture, and the image of one who revels in her new role was well captured.

Unfortunately the Princess is not without her critics, as the sensations in 1985 over her father's wartime role in the SS, and her alleged affair with an American millionaire, so disastrously proved. Those stories and their aftermath may have reduced her faith in human charity, but she is strong enough to be able to continue to develop her life in her own enthusiastic way.

Queen Mother, but the previous month it was announced that she would not be available, and the engagement was hastily tacked on to the Princess of Wales' schedule. As it happened it was an apt enough alternative. The Princess had early in February assumed the presidency of five organisations, four of them orientated towards benefiting young people, and one of them was the Albany Trust.

The Albany Trust is one of those little-known, very localised charities which achieve any degree of celebrity only on an occasion such as this. In fact it has long been associated with

Prompted in no small measure by a spell of warm weather, a colourful carnival atmosphere permeated the South East London suburb of Deptford when on 18th May the Princess of Wales performed the last of her official engagements before the birth of Prince William. She was there to open a new community centre, erected at a cost of almost £3 million through the good offices of the Albany Trust. The opening was to have been performed by the

the Royal Family – indeed it began under the auspices of none other than H.R.H. the Duchess of Albany. She was the wife of Queen Victoria's youngest, and only haemophiliac, son Prince Leopold (1853-1884), who in

1881 was created Duke of Albany. A homely, good-natured woman, she devoted her life to good causes, particularly after the death of her husband, to whom she had been married for less than three years.

One cause she espoused with

Eventually the exploitation was halted, but the Duchess and the Minister found that they had, well-meaningly but unwittingly, created their own little unemployment problem. With the prospect of seeing the girls on the streets making their own dubious efforts to employ themselves gainfully, the Duchess decided to put right the mischief she had created, and in 1894 established a Trust, which has borne her name ever since, designed to cater for the girls in their long hours of enforced idleness.

When the Duchess, whose sister Queen Emma was the great-

her inimitable brand of crusading zeal was against the exploitation of adolescent girls in the Deptford area, who at a time of considerable poverty and squalor were being employed in slaughter-houses and in the rag trade for scandalously low rates of pay. The Duchess spent much of her time trying to locate the Whitehall official who might be able to put a stop to the practice, and finally found a Minister whom she knew well enough to persuade to take up the cudgels on her behalf.

grandmother of the present Queen Beatrix of the Netherlands, died in 1922, her only daughter, the late Princess Alice, Countess of Athlone, took over the presidency, which she held until her own death fifty-nine years later at the age of 97. That was in January 1981. Two years earlier she had button-holed her great-great-nephew Prince Charles and persuaded him to lay the foundation stone of the Community Centre which his wife was now in Deptford to open formally (these pages).

The Princess of Wales spent over an hour at the centre, receiving the usual heaps of posies from the crowds she spoke to during the visit, and looking at her most contented. She did not, however, forgo any opportunity to sit down nor, as one might have come by now to expect, to talk about babies. With her own confinement

expected only six weeks later, the creche was the focus of great interest. She also met those who give their time voluntarily to help in the centre, watched a group of pensioners at a bingo session and visited the centre's restaurant – and it was here that mothers and children heard of the latest preparations for the royal birth.

The stories didn't quite tally and no-one was quite sure whether the Princess said that her baby *would* be a boy or that she hoped it would. "We'll just have to wait and see," she finally told 14-year-old David Rowland. She took one look at Mrs Patricia Woodgates' five-month-old twins and confessed "I don't think I could cope with a brace. I only hope I can cope with one

when the time comes." Mrs Woodgates warned her that "you don't learn much about them until you've actually had them," a remark that put into perspective the Princess' revelation to Mrs Doreen Markland, that Prince Charles had been studying books about pregnancy and baby care so feverishly of late that he had become "something of an expert. He keeps telling me what to do," she added, "and I don't like it!"

The visit came to an end with

the presentation to the Princess of a picture of the community centre drawn by Mr Reg Rowlands, the Chairman of the New Cross Building Society. The old Duchess of Albany would have been proud of her achievement.

With official engagements over until October (as it was then thought) the Princess was expected to remain out of public sight for the foreseeable future. The precedent which had always

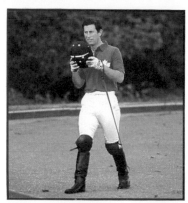

(these pages) in which he played for the Canadian side run by the biscuit heir Mr Galen Weston. It wasn't, however, the best of days: the wind was chilly and she ventured only short distances from the car, where she frequently sheltered, looking just a little bored.

kept royal ladies discreetly indoors during the visible stages of their pregnancies had already been broken and many people expected that time would now be called. But the Princess of Wales has not been called innovatory for nothing and she turned up in public almost as often as there was a polo match to see in which Prince Charles was playing. Giving the lie to the widely believed story, created out of her reactions to some pretty terrifying scenes on the field in 1981, that she disliked polo, she followed Prince Charles almost everywhere, pacing the perimeters with the informality for which she has become well known.

Thus on 22nd May she travelled with the Prince to Windsor Great Park for a weekend game

They change the Guard here, ambassadors are officially accredited here, an obscure Epiphany service is held in its chapel once a year, and in the old days Royal Levées were held here in what was then called "the Season."
One could be readily forgiven for supposing that, as far as official or public appearances are concerned, the Royal Family seems to take a dim view of St James's, and give it a wide berth.

Thank you
TO THE READERS OF:-
woman
FOR OUR SUNSHINE COACH
From the children of
...CHINGTON COURT SCHOOL
...OUSE SCHOOL

St James's Palace is one of the more obscure of London's royal buildings. Not physically, for its long, Georgian-windowed walls can be skirted at any time of day by anyone wishing to get from Trafalgar Square to Piccadilly by road. But for all the security surrounding it, Buckingham Palace is known far more intimately than St James's. As the diplomatic focal point of the royal connection, St James's wears a reputation even more forbidding than its dark frontage.

Visits by its members are conspicuous by their rarity. The occasional concert, exhibition or fashion show is staged here from time to time, and may draw a royal audience or patron. This was where the Prince and Princess of Wales exhibited their wedding presents during two hectic and profitable months in 1981, and where Prince and Princess Michael of Kent have had their two children christened. Like every State Visitor to this country before

and since, the visiting Sultan of Oman came here to receive addresses of welcome in March 1982.
Both the Duke of Kent and his sister Princess Alexandra have their London offices here, and for the Kents, York House at the western end of the Palace is their official London residence.
So the Duchess of Kent did not have very far to come when on the morning of 24th May she made a very special presentation to fifty handicapped children.

Yard was spectacularly exciting. Each coach was festooned with balloons and streamers and would shortly take them all on a tour of London before their journeys back to their home towns.

The Duchess found the occasion both moving and enjoyable. With her well-earned reputation for being very much at home with children, she was irresistably drawn to these youngsters whose happiness

The Variety Club of Great Britain, which justly boasts of being the greatest children's charity in the world, had recently completed a massive fund-raising exercise to provide its famous Sunshine Coaches for the children of three schools in Bradford, Bristol and Seaford, Sussex. For handicapped children, outdoor activities are a vital part of the school curriculum and their first sight of their new means of indispensible transport arriving into Stable

depends so heavily on the goodwill of others. As she waved the last of the coaches off (above), their passengers carried with them special memories of their very royal day.

It all made for one of the happier and lighter sides of the otherwise very solemn, dignified and diplomatic character which traditionally surrounds the Court of St James's.

A five-week season of
Tchaikovsky's "Swan Lake,"
performed at the London
Coliseum by the London
Festival Ballet, came to a royal
climax on 25th May when the
Ballet's Patron, Princess
Margaret, attended a gala
performance in aid of its
Development Fund. This new
production by John Field was
certain to attract the Princess'
attention: she has maintained a
lifelong interest in the ballet –
she became the first President of
the newly formed Royal Ballet in
1957 as part of her more general
musical appreciation. Music and
its interpretation in the wider
arts have been important to her,

continued to be well aired in
public, with less private matters
again distinguished by varying
degrees of controversy.
The publication in October of
Nigel Dempster's biography
"HRH The Princess Margaret:
A Life Unfulfilled" contained a
detailed résumé of material the
author had previously disclosed
in his *Daily Mail* gossip column,
and more. It was said to have
been read in draft and approved
by the Princess, but her former
husband, Lord Snowdon,
dismissed it as having been
"written without interviews."
Jocelyn Stevens, a friend of the
Princess, weighed in, detailing
its many inaccuracies in an

as she disclosed in the BBC
programme "Desert Island
Discs" in 1981, when she
selected favourite recordings of
ballet music as well as jazz and
opera.
The Princess had undertaken,
in the previous 12 months,
her usual quota of public
engagements – including visits
abroad to attend the Diamond
Jubilee of King Sobhuza II of
Swaziland in September, to
confer independence in Antigua
in November, and to open an art
exhibition at Houston, Texas in
February. But she will, if she
cares to, remember it as a time
when issues in her private life

article in the *Daily Express* – a paper which itself ran a week-long serialisation about her, in competition with the book's serialisation in the *Daily Mail.* The statement in the book that she "would like to marry again" seemed to be confirmed by the many sightings of her with the 55-year-old widower Norman Lonsdale. They were photographed together at a inasked ball in November; he stayed with her on Mustique in February; and when the Princess was spotted wearing an unfamiliar ring on her engagement finger during an official visit to Glasgow in April, the rumour-mongers drew their

barred for the third time in four unhappy years from attending the Christmas Ball at Keele University of which she was Chancellor: nothing personal here; it was just that the left wingers in the Students' Union took objection to the police prowling around before and during royal visits. And she received her annual insult from Willie Hamilton MP who called her "a useless, middle-aged floozie" in front of 200 nurses and hospital workers as part of their campaign for higher pay. Sometimes she must wonder whether it's all worth it. Who'd be a Princess?

conclusions. They were almost actively encouraged by tantalisingly ambiguous statements by both Mr Lonsdale and the Princess' private secretary, but when two days later HRH turned up at an NSPCC lunch with *three* rings on her engagement finger, and unreserved denials were issued all round, the story magically vanished.

For good measure, the Princess was criticised quite severely for refusing – apparently on the grounds that it would spoil her hair-do – to wear a sterile hairnet at a medical products factory in Plymouth. She was

On 27th May, a welcome splash of colour on a drab day was provided by the comings and goings at Westminster Abbey where the Queen installed the latest crop of Knights Grand

is cocooned in time and place. In time, it is a comparatively short ritual surrounded by a grandiose religious service full of trumpetings, psalms of praise, patriotic music and the constant shifting of beadles, almsmen, genealogists and Scarlet Rod. In place, it happens in the inner sanctum of the Order's own chapel, the King Henry VII Chapel, away from the eyes of established Knights in the body of the Abbey.

Like most occasions of high ceremony, precision is of the essence. Gentlemen at Arms and Yeomen of the Guard officially took up positions at 10.57 am; Princess Alice arrived (bottom, far right and opposite page bottom left) with her lady in waiting Miss Jane Egerton-Warburton at 11.05; Prince Charles – Grand Master since

Cross of the Order of the Bath. As Sovereign of the Order she presided at this irregularly-staged embodiment of a tradition formalised in 1725. For, unlike the Garter Service, this is not an annual event: this year's ceremony was held to install those Knights appointed since 1978. There were eleven of them – five generals, four air marshals, an admiral and Lord Adeane, the Queen's former private secretary. Fortunately for all of them the bathing rite, from which the Order takes its title, has long since been dropped, though George I included it in the schedule of obligatory ceremonies on creating the Order out of the old medieval "Degree of Knighthood." The installation ceremony itself

who, as Grand Master, delivers it to the Senior of the Knights to be installed, so that they can all take the oath. This includes an undertaking to "defend maidens, widows and orphans in their rights and . . . suffer no extortion."

The Grand Master has then to seat the new Knights in their

stalls, but no sooner is this done than they have to rise again to go and stand beneath their respective banners.

Another pattern of synchronised movement precedes the Queen's obeisance before the altar as she offers gold and silver, as does the senior of the new Knights. There follows a ritual drawing and sheathing of swords, and exhortations to defend the Gospel and maintain the "Sovereign's Right and Honour," before the select gathering returns to rejoin the congregation.

A general thanksgiving and prayers are followed by the Blessing and the National Anthem, and the procession out through the East Cloister begins (left and far left). And a few words from the Queen and Prince Charles (opposite page) to a cluster of school-children convinces them that these robed and tiara'd figures with their magical symbols are pleasantly human after all.

1975 – arrived (left) at 11.09; and the Queen (far right) at 11.12.

The service takes much the same form as any Morning Service, with psalm, lesson, versicles and responses, prayers and anthems. Then a thin procession of royalty and Knights moves up the Abbey past the High Altar and into the King Henry VII Chapel, while anthems are sung. Once inside the Chapel the members of the procession take their appointed places – the Queen and Prince Charles have special stalls – and sit, except for the Knights about to be installed, who remain standing. Bath King of Arms receives a Book of Statutes from the Deputy Secretary and proceeds towards Prince Charles

There is nothing particularly new about the Queen of the United Kingdom meeting the Holy Father. Elizabeth II has met a succession of Popes – as Princess Elizabeth she was received by Pope Pius XII, and as Queen she called on Pope John XXIII in 1961, and on the present Pope in 1980 during each of her State Visits to Italy. Since Henry VIII broke with the Church of Rome, however, no

Pope has ever set foot inside the United Kingdom, far less parleyed with the Sovereign. For that reason His Holiness' forty minutes with Her Majesty at Buckingham Palace on 28th May 1982 was one of the most historically significant events of her reign. As a meeting between Heads of State it was all a matter of ordinary diplomatic courtesy, but as a symbol of the coming together of two churches, whose rupture over four hundred years ago still excites powerful controversy, it had a potency all its own.

That was particularly so in the light of further controversy stirred up by news of his impending visit: the Orange Order branded the Queen as a potential "traitor to the Constitution" and Mr Enoch Powell said it was "constitutionally and logically impossible for England to contain both the Queen and the Pope." Then further difficulties arose with the Falklands crisis, the Argentinians claiming that the visit would bestow the unfair advantage of Papal blessing upon the British cause.

This led to a further confusion. Originally, to appease the ultra-

Protestants it had been stated that the meeting was not between Heads of Churches but between Heads of State. When the Falklands crisis became an issue the Argentinians were told that the meeting had no political, but only a religious, significance.

The Pope mollified the Argentinians by promising to visit them in June, and his tour of Britain and meeting with the Queen passed off quietly and satisfactorily. The Pope was met at the Palace by an official (far left) but the Queen came out to the Grand Entrance to bid him farewell personally.

"Buckingham Palace – June 2: The Queen accompanied by the Duke of Edinburgh, Queen Elizabeth the Queen Mother, Princess Anne Mrs Mark Phillips, The Duke and Duchess of Gloucester, Prince and Princess Michael of Kent and Princess Alexander (sic) the Hon Mrs Angus Ogilvy and the Hon Mr Angus Ogilvy, honoured Epsom Races with her presence today."

It's a bit of a mouthful, even for the Court Circular, but as usual it relates only the bare facts of attendance or presence, and in this case without the additional details of how they all got there, what they did when they arrived, or how they travelled back. But

breed and race a Derby winner still continues, has rarely missed this most prestigious of the world's classic races and the most financially rewarding of the British classics. And it is a rare occasion when the majority of the Royal family do not accompany her.

more conservatively, wore her complete outfit of matching hat, coat and dress. Princess Anne was in a fresh, green dress, while the Duchess of Gloucester preferred bright white. Princess Michael at Epsom was indistinguishable from Princess Michael at Royal Ascot, with her stately

of arms or crowns affixed to their roofs. It was sudden and violent, as if to remind everyone who had come to enjoy this annual beano that the Falklands were closer than they might have thought. It sent some 300,000 people scurrying for shelter – girls in bikinis or ra-ras looked

then everyone knows that the Royal Family habitually have a ripping time at Epsom – it's almost as imperative as solemnity at the Opening of Parliament or hats at Ascot. The Queen, whose quest to

This year the Queen arrived coatless – unusually for her but the weather in the first week of June had for once turned up trumps and the sun beat down relentlessly for most of the afternoon. The Queen Mother,

ensemble and grand feathered hat.

A thunderstorm broke just after the impressive royal arrival – a procession of Rolls Royces purring up the course with badges displaying personal coats

never so out of place beneath picnic rugs and newspapers, and grown men, stripped to the waist and covered in sun tan oil, cowered under the nearest umbrellas.

An hour before the big race it all

stopped and the sun rejuvenated the festival atmosphere. Eventually the Royal party came down from the stand and inspected the 1982 Derby runners from the side of the course (bottom picture, the Queen Mother and the Queen with – left to right – Mr Ogilvy, Princess Alexandra, Prince Philip and – at the back in the centre – the Duke of Gloucester). As the expressions on the royal faces made clear, all were fascinated by the procession of these finely groomed horses cantering by at the peak of their fitness and form. They returned to the Royal Box where their every

The Queen had a cup of tea there and made a close inspection of the contents of the flower box. The 1982 Derby was as exciting, both in anticipation and on the day itself, as almost any of the two hundred-odd meetings of past years. The prize to the eventual winner was higher than ever, and the value in international stud fees would be phenomenal. Yet, for once, there were no royal histrionics or the customary excited gesticulations as the runners came home. The Queen's personal interest seemed more dispassionate than in previous years. Perhaps that was because, in the hour of war, Peacetime only came seventh.

gesture could be watched: Princess Anne discussed with her father (opposite page, left), the Queen with her mother (opposite page, right) and Princess Michael with everyone (above and centre pictures).

Or perhaps because, as Susan Sangster's horse Golden Fleece ran in the winner, the Queen knew she had yet another year to wait before her chance came up again.

This was one of the last public appearances the Princess of Wales made before the birth of her baby and she might justifiably have looked back on it all with a degree of satisfaction. It had been a public, almost as

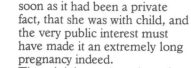

soon as it had been a private fact, that she was with child, and the very public interest must have made it an extremely long pregnancy indeed.

Though it began in a glow of public congratulation – the Lord Mayor of London likened the news to a hallmark on the gold ingot of the Royal Wedding, and the Prince of Wales praised "the wonderful effect my dear wife has had on everyone" – excesses of publicity threatened at times to turn the whole thing sour and cause the mother-to-be to modify her flexible, informal approach to her royal duties. Over-zealous photographers plagued her at Highgrove and Tetbury and again on the

Bahamian holiday, and were rebuked by the Queen for doing so. Even the BBC was considered to have gone too far with a comedy sketch showing the Princess giving evidence in a court case against a contraceptive firm. Rumours abounded that American and British firms were in the process of making feature films about her courtship with the Prince of Wales, one of them containing "details not revealed before," but the finished products were bland and disappointing.

Artists had a field day. Bryan Organ's official painting of the Princess was slashed at the National Portrait Gallery, where it now hangs restored and protected by Perspex. The wedding was celebrated on canvas by Sue Ryder, who portrayed the Princess in a froth of light, filmy bridal silk, but avoiding over-sentimentality. Ruskin Spear painted the Prince

and Princess kissing on Buckingham Palace balcony, but over-emphasised what was in reality a fleeting peck almost into a clinch. Carol Payne went one worse and exhibited a painting at Plymouth showing

the royal couple in more intimate surroundings.

The speculation about twins must have sickened her at times. The baby's sex was universally discussed and the general plumping for a boy proved

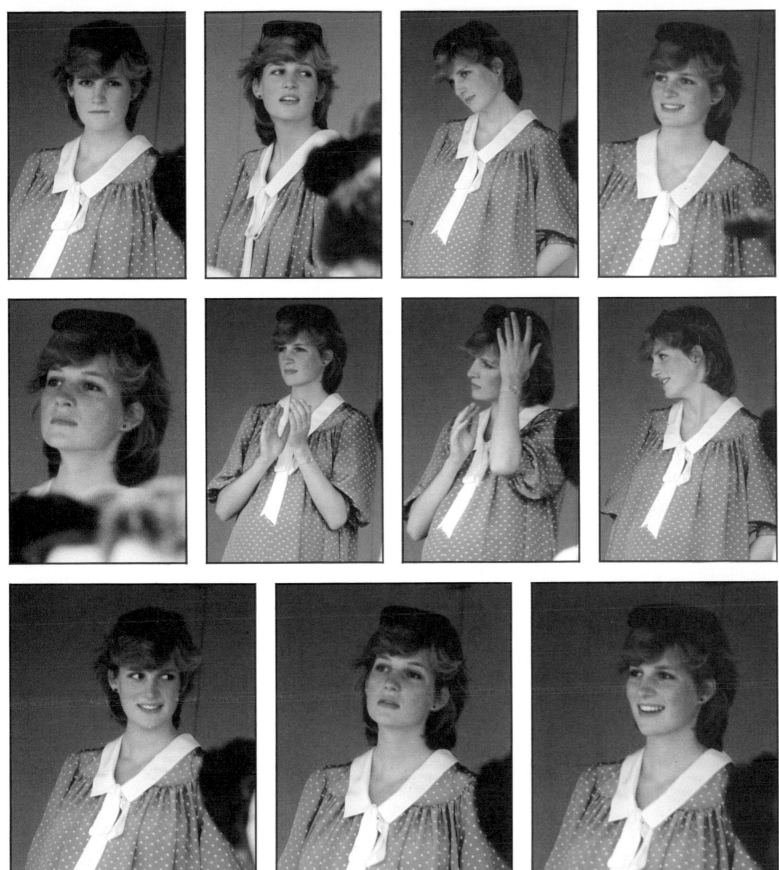

inspired. The place of its birth divided the country – Highgrove, Buckingham Palace and St Mary's Paddington were all candidates. The suppliers of baby clothes, maternity wear, nursery furniture, equipment and toys, became the target of endless Press detective work. (Incidentally, the doll trade was

she was widely reported to have taken on the Queen over whether her baby should accompany her on future royal tours abroad. And she appears to have chosen the baby's nanny herself.

If one thing is totally beyond doubt it is that the codes of public behaviour as they affect

thrilled: "This is definitely the year of the baby doll," said one manufacturer.) Even the Princess' own bedroom, with the chance of housing a four-poster bed more than once slept in by the French courtesan, Diane de Poitiers, excited interest.

If ever the Princess had properly acquired an image, it changed over this period. She seemed less vulnerable than before her marriage and rumours that she was decisive, unyielding, even precociously ambitious began to spread. Certainly photographers caught her more than once letting everyone know of some displeasure. In five months she was held responsible for having sacked Prince Charles' valet and two of her own detectives and

princes and princesses of the Blood Royal and their spouses have changed fundamentally and irrevocably. From the relative obscurity of a position as the youngest daughter of an Earl, the Princess has become the wife of the heir to the Throne, but she has brought to the monarchy as an institution all the best elements of uninhibited social and personal behaviour. It raised eyebrows at first, this free and easy chat with the common herd, this touching of other people's babies, those giggling larks with young children. But no chord with the public was more sympathetically struck, and no more timely boost to the

monarchy's popularity was ever so comprehensively furnished or maintained. And all, it seems, without effort.

That statement may imply that it is easy to "become" a member of the Royal Family and to assimilate its ways, its taboos, its "image." That may or may not be the case – only the Princess herself and her mentor Lady Susan Hussey can verify, and for obvious reasons they are not available for comment. It probably comes nearer the truth to say that the Princess has modified what everybody thought was the fixed, unchanging manner of royalty whenever it appeared in public. If so she is accomplishing this not through perversity or even as the result of a conscious decision. She has clearly accepted Prince Charles' hand in marriage and the monarchy's soul for life on terms which reflect her own uncomplicated values as much as the institution's complexities and quaintness. The public have been easily won over, and the Royal Family is demonstrably not far behind.

If truth be told it was not actually completed until 1692 but the 66 acres of land were bought in 1682 and work on the institution "for the relief of such Land Souldiers . . . lame or infirme in the Service of the Crowne" began the same year. Its full name, the Royal Hospital, derives from its founding by King Charles II, the "Merry Monarch," whose restoration in 1660 led the monarchist, and in events somewhat reactionary, backlash against the austerities of Puritan Britain.

The annual parade has for decades enjoyed royal patronage

Thursday 10th June 1982 was a day of anniversaries. Eight years before, the Duke of Gloucester, the last surviving child of King George V, died. It was also Prince Philip's sixty-first birthday: guns boomed again in Hyde Park and at the Tower; flags fluttered brightly from public buildings. Which was nice because it was also the day on which the Queen, as a special mark of her affection for the Chelsea Pensioners, chose to celebrate with them the three hundredth anniversary of the founding of their Hospital.

and this special royal visit added calibre and a grand sense of occasion to the colourful vision of the lines of red-coated in-pensioners (above) and the Romanesque statue of "our Pious Founder," swathed in oak leaves (top left) as a reminder of his hiding place after the Battle of Worcester in 1651. Figure Court was alive with the shuffle

of scarlet, the winking of a thousand medals, the brisk pacings of commanding officers in black, and the gentler sociable movements of the Queen. Dressed in a soft mauve outfit that was to become a favourite this summer, she reviewed 436 men, the able-bodied during the marchpast (above) and the others sitting on benches, black tricornes nodding and walking-sticks wagging as they hoped for the chance of a word with the Queen as she passed (right and below right).

It is a sobering thought that at 99 years of age, one of them could claim to have served in the Boer War in the last dim glimmer of the reign of her great-great-grandmother Queen Victoria. Others took part in campaigns in India as far back as 1908. Over a hundred of the Hospital's present complement served in the First World War, and nearly 250 in the Second. The roll call of their foreign service recall Britain's inter-war

imperial interests – Palestine, Iraq, East Africa and Aden. Between them, the in-pensioners share no fewer than 250 gallantry medals and awards for outstanding service, from the Order of the British Empire to the Belgian Albert Medal. King Charles II's foundation of the Hospital grew out of his recognition of the importance of his army. He would be gratified by the knowledge that after three hundred years the Hospital, and the royal connection, were still thriving.

There were no new Knights of the Order of the Garter to be invested in 1982, so the Throne Room of Windsor Castle was bereft of ceremony on 14th June. But there was a meeting of the Order, as usual, and a luncheon at which all the Knights taking part in the afternoon's service were present, along with the officers of the Order and the pages.

If it is ever permissible to talk of the Garter ceremony as low-key, that year's proceedings fitted the description. Relatively speaking of course. The ceremonial is in essence as spectacular, the

colour as vivid, the applause as warm as always, but there was no doubt that some earlier ceremonies had the edge. The buzz of speculation centred first and foremost on the Princess of Wales: she was here last year as Lady Diana Spencer – would she attend again today in her new capacity? Spectators craned their necks and swore they'd seen her, but in fact she never appeared. No foreign royalty either. Two years before both the Queen of Denmark and the Grand Duke of Luxemburg had attended, to add their own brand of informality on the

windswept steps of St George's Chapel. Today it was as if King Farouk's prophecy – "One day there will be only five kings left – of Britain, hearts, clubs, diamonds and spades" – had come true.

Even the Duke of Edinburgh was absent: at short notice he had left London Airport that morning to attend the funeral of King Khalid of Saudi Arabia – a State Visitor to Britain in 1981 – who had died the previous day, and to pay his respects and convey the Queen's condolences to his brother and successor Crown-Prince Faud.

Thus, for once, the Queen walked alone in the procession which formed inside the Castle and snaked down the Grand Staircase to the Grand Entrance where the ten Military Knights of Windsor, in scarlet tunics with white sashes, and the thirteen tabarded heralds and pursuivants joined to form the vanguard of the procession. Between them and the Sovereign came eighteen

Knights, incredibly resplendent in their heavy, rich, blue mantles and white plumes shifting restlessly in a stiffish, though by no means unpleasant breeze. Sir Harold Wilson – one of the few recognisable faces, or names for that matter – waved cheerily, even royally. He was the only one to do so, as if all the applause were being accorded exclusively to him. The Knights were followed by the Queen Mother, with the Prince of Wales as her escort, and the applause grew pointedly louder.

The Queen, her face almost framed by the sweeping lines of

Coronation much of its distinctive and memorable flavour. It lasted an hour and included an ethereal, florid motet setting of one of the Psalms – a Latin elegiac version of Psalm 150 by the sixteenth-century organist and composer William Byrd.

The procession back was more, and less, spectacular than the arrival. More, because the Royal Family used carriages to take them back up the hill to the Castle: the Queen was joined by the Prince of Wales, the Queen Mother by the Duke of Beaufort. Less, because the

her plumed cap, looked defiantly young and palpably happy in the leisurely walk towards St George's Chapel as, section by section, the thousands of spectators, ticket-holders and invitees, rose to applaud her as they had done her mother and son. Soldiers of the Life Guards and the Blues and Royals, distinguishable by their white and red plumes respectively, studded the route on either side.

The service was relayed to those outside through unseen loudspeakers, and was full of the sounds – like Walton's *Te Deum* and Gordon Jacob's National Anthem – which gave the

Rome, nor the demotion by the Vatican of the Order's patron saint, St George, nor the scepticism of a generation speeding on towards the twenty-first century, have diminished the pleasurable tradition of its virtually annual celebration.

The week ushered in by the splendour of the Garter ceremony continued with splendour of another kind, difficult to regard as formal and official, but as inescapably British as any military parade. On the Tuesday following Garter Day and for the three remaining days of the week, the eyes of the horse-racing fraternity were turned to, and fixed on, Royal Ascot.

Not only the horse-racing fraternity of course. Royal Ascot is as synonymous with hats as with horses and the expectation of four days of seeing and being seen on Ascot's sweeping course-side lawns or in its

Knights, few of them in the flower of youth, took cars. And eventually the Guards arranged themselves back into units and marched off as well.

Edward III had, for most of his comparatively long life, a sense of proportion, and would have been more than surprised to know that the Order of the Garter which, according to legend, he founded after picking up a lady's garter and placing it, jokingly, upon his own leg, was still alive and flourishing in the dying years of the twentieth century. Neither the breach with

fashionable bars and restaurants is as likely to draw any socialite or sartorial expert as is the opportunity to be in the unsaddling enclosure when the Gold Cup winner comes in.

Any venture into the social scene in Britain leads to excess and the unavoidable juggernaut of commercial marketing makes it chic to run publicity stunts against the respectable and respected Ascot background. Thus the camera crews are always looking for Mrs Shilling in her outrageous creations, or spying on some advertising

Anne who directed the laying-out of the Ascot course almost three hundred years ago and the presence of her equally enthusiastic successor today symbolises the continuing, though not unbroken, equestrian sympathies for which the Royal Family is well-known.

The Queen's continued patronage of the event also embodies a social statement of precedence and authority within that now amorphous section of society which is content to look to her for an indefinable leadership, an annual stamp of approval and encouragement for

agency's furtive attempts to place models in the correct setting as they brandish glasses of wine, sport summer fashions or purse lips caked with the latest cosmetic preparation. It is hard to see where the Royal Family might fit into this, but its members enter into the four-day festival with as much gusto, in their restrained royal way, as anyone. It was of course Queen

the respectable in a world where respectability enjoys a declining role.

The grand entrance and arrival say it all. A line of carriages bowls at casual pace through Ascot's famous Golden Gates and an unstoppable surge of people rushes towards the rails for a fleeting glimpse of the procession, thin and silent in an immensely wide expanse of turf, being hauled by. Similarly, a crowd of spectators in the Royal Enclosure makes way for the royal progress on foot to the Royal Box in the Queen Elizabeth II Stand, and the front

Queen Mother looking like – well, looking like the Queen Mother, in her favourite pale coats and chiffon dresses. Prince Philip missed out on Tuesday and Friday; Princess Margaret wore her azalea Royal Wedding outfit and made nonsense of the rumours that she is no friend of the éclatante Princess Michael (opposite page, centre), and it was so very easy to see why the Duchess of Kent has been described as one of the seven most sophisticated women in the world.

lines of ladies in competing hats compete also for the chance to catch the royal eye (opposite page, bottom right).

From 15th to 18th June the ritual was enacted again before crowds whose numbers promised to exceed the record. More hopes of seeing the Princess of Wales perhaps? If so they were disappointed. On no day did she join the carriage procession and only on one did she slip quietly into the Royal Box, having arrived unobtrusively by car. In fact there was no day when the Family was wholly represented. The Queen and Queen Mother attended on all four days, the Queen looking particularly chic in a beige-coloured scalloped coat and matching hat, and the

Like all other members of the Royal Family, the Queen and Prince Philip pay several visits to Scotland in the course of the year, in addition to the long summer holiday at Balmoral and their occasional Spring weekends there. It has long been a custom, however, for them to spirit was enormously helped by the installation of the railways, of which she made such comprehensive use that the steam engine might seem to have been invented specifically for her.

During this week, the Queen and her husband reside

acknowledge this part of the kingdom by a special week-long visit, with each day packed with engagements taking them to all parts of the lowlands. This practice has its origins in Queen Victoria's reign. Her personal love of Scotland prompted her to make frequent visits north of the Border, and her pioneering permanently at their official residence in Scotland, the Palace of Holyroodhouse, and the Queen's personal bodyguard for the duration is the three hundred-year-old Royal Company of Archers.

Scotland, which was the first part of the United Kingdom

Cathedral Edinburgh at which two new Knights of the Order of the Thistle were installed – Lord Elgin and Lord Thompson. The Service, which is an annual one, took place in the Order's Chapel which occupies a small extension to the Cathedral, and the ceremonial included the

formation of the Royal Company of Archers as the Queen's bodyguard, and music from the band of the Gordon Highlanders.

The visual impact of the Thistle ceremony (this page) is similar to that of the Garter, although the surroundings – Parliament

Square in Edinburgh – are not so imposing as Windsor Castle. But the rich, flowing robes are there, the handsome white plumes are there, and the long stately procession of Knights follows a pattern similar to the Windsor ceremony. Unlike Windsor, however, the Thistle service is held in the morning, with the traditional luncheon taking place at Holyroodhouse afterwards.

The Order of the Thistle has its roots in the 15th century, but Queen Anne made the last of several revivals in 1703.

officially to greet the Queen during her Silver Jubilee tour of 1977, always looks forward to these days each year when the Sovereign's attention is concentrated solely on matters north of the Border. At no time is the excitement and sense of national identity greater than when the royal couple attend the Pipers' Ball and the great ceremonies of the Order of the Thistle.

In 1982 the Pipers' Ball, or the Royal Scottish Pipers' Society Ball, to give it its full name, celebrated its centenary and the Assembly Rooms in royal Edinburgh looked especially festive. The Queen and Prince Philip are seen (left) arriving, on 2nd July, accompanied by the Chairman of the Centenary Committee, and (centre left) with Sir James Morrison-Low, the Society's Honorary Pipe-Major.

Earlier that day the Queen and Duke of Edinburgh had attended a service in St Giles'

William.
The Duchess' visit to Stoneleigh came two days before she and the Duke celebrated their tenth wedding anniversary. They still share the modest, retiring sort of nature which craves obscurity and the peace of the countryside, and which – by some accounts – prompted them to plan setting up home on the Isle of Dogs before Prince William's early and tragic death at the age of 30 left them with the prospect, which soon materialised, of public duty for life. In 1983, Princess Alice paid tribute to their dedication. "They work incomparably harder than we did before the war," she wrote. "But," she added, as an example of relative financial strictures, "for much of his day's business, the Duke dodges about London on a motorbike."

The Duchess of Gloucester was among the visitors to the Royal Show on 6th July, touring part of the massive site which for many years has found a permanent home at Stoneleigh in Warwickshire. No branch of the Royal Family is more readily associated with farming than the Gloucesters. The late Duke ran farms at the country home, Barnwell Manor in Northamptonshire, in partnership with his wife, Princess Alice, and their elder son Prince

(these pages) she was in the Home Counties, visiting Croham Hurst Place, a home for the Blind at Sanderstead in Surrey. This was one of her last public

As patron of the London Association of the Blind, Princess Alexandra attended its 125th Anniversary celebrations early in July. On 27th July

duties before a two-month summer break. A new schedule of appointments beginning in October included a ten-day visit to Thailand as the guest of King Bhumibhol and Queen Sirikit, for the 200th anniversary celebrations of the Chakri

dynasty. Princess Alexandra's son James took a family photograph marking his parents' departure for Bangkok: a keen photographer, he used an automatic release so that he could be included in the picture along with his parents and sister Marina.

regatta. Taking the helm in the Yeoman class yacht which has served him for many years, and casting only an occasional, furtively suspicious eye at the photographers (below) he crossed the line in second place, only 90 seconds behind the winning craft, Highland Fling. After attending a Royal London Yacht Club reception and a Royal Yacht Squadron Ball at Cowes Castle the following day, he boarded the Royal Yacht *Britannia* on 3rd August for Balmoral, and another Highland fling, before visiting Holland to compete in the World Driving Championships.

The Queen has occasionally been there, Prince Charles has often raced and windsurfed there, Princess Anne and Prince Edward used to sail there and Princess Alexandra and her husband Mr Angus Ogilvy were frequent spectators there. But Prince Philip is the one member of the Royal Family for whom attendance at part of Cowes Week at least is an annual event. He was there again on 1st August, competing for the Queen's Cup – the major award in the Royal Southampton Yacht Club's opening

to go the way of many of his other outdoor interests, it was a day when he wore two teams' shirts – one for the Maple Leaf team, and one for Les Diables Bleus – and had no inhibitions about changing them in public. Nor did he think twice about

The Princess of Wales, keeping a low profile save for one official appearance at the Falklands service in London a few days before, was absent from Cowdray Park in Sussex on 2nd August. For her husband, whose enthusiasm for polo has refused

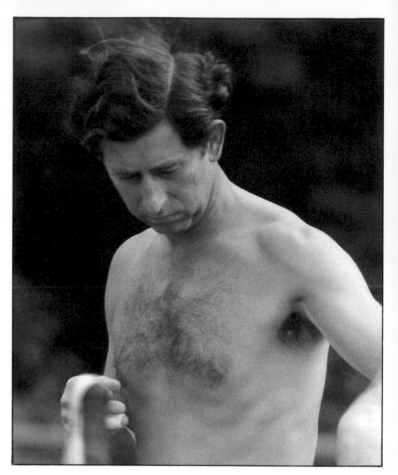

dodging behind the most convenient hedge to answer the inevitable call of nature as inconspicuously as possible (far right), nor again about nailing the old myth that royalty is not to be seen with glass in hand, let alone drinking from it (opposite page, top left). This was one of his last

adventures on the polo field. By the middle of August he and the Princess had made for Balmoral to join the Queen on her annual Highland holiday, leaving the English polo season to play out its last couple of weeks. Normally that would have meant no more polo for almost ten months, but in the event his tour of Australia in March 1983 gave him the opportunity to

limber up again for a couple of matches at Warwick Farm near Sydney. Understandably he found himself a little rusty after seven months off the field, but nevertheless contrived to be on the winning side on both occasions, justifying his commendable handicap of four with some well-praised shots, yet unable to avoid one of those legendary falls from the saddle.

The Queen closed the Commonwealth Games on 9th October and the competitions seemed almost incidental by then. In a thrilling afternoon's finals England, thanks partly to a wonderful 1,500 metre run by Steve Cram (above), nudged Australia off the top of the overall medals table. Keith Connor's triple jump was the second longest in history. Raelene Boyle retired amid unending praise and applause. The day's weather, performance and spirit were perfect. The Queen had time to enjoy it – and record it (right) – before pronouncing the closing words (above left). Matilda, winking coquettishly at all and sundry, was the most popular feature, even when swathed in coloured smoke from the Chinese dragon (left). The Queen even told her driver to slow down for her own final lap of honour.

"If it's Tuesday, it must be Tuvalu," was certainly not one of the Queen's thoughts as she approached the island of Funafuti, capital of the former Ellice Islands. In a life where the well-prepared and even the spectacular may seem routine, there was nothing remotely mundane about the start – nor indeed the end – of her two-day visit, beginning on 26th October to Tuvalu. There is a harbour here, and the royal barge might have used it, but conditions were good enough for a more distinctive welcome. The barge was met by a flotilla of long canoes, whose paddlers were charged with the duty of conveying the Queen, Prince Philip and their party to the shore (opposite page, top). The canoes – built in a week, of light hardwood called puka, and costing no more than $270 (about £150) – were copies of those used locally for skipjack fishing, but the bright colours of protective paint marked their special purpose today.

That night the celebrations continued. The Queen and Prince Philip were back in the maneapa for a traditional feast, served in an equally traditional manner. In a carefully rehearsed procession, bearers brought an amazing selection of food – legs of pork, quarters of chicken, crabs, lobsters and fish, even cooked blackbirds and bats, a whole succession of vegetables and fruit from the huge taros, or sweet potatoes, to the clusters of small bananas. The

Queen was visibly uncertain how to tackle this enormous spread, and seemed self-consciously to inspect and study its constituents, rather than to taste them. Prince Philip had no such reservations, and joked happily with his serving girl as he tucked into a variety of dishes. Afterwards, a ceremonial crowning, in which all the guests received decorative circlets of flowers, left the Queen with a cluster of densely arranged frangipani on her head, and the Duke with a more rakish version of straw and flame tree blooms on his – a result at which the Duke was openly amused (opposite page). This ceremony heralded the beginning of the evening's entertainment, and the Queen and Prince Philip moved from this table (far right) to watch a three-hour programme of non-stop singing. Every one of Tuvalu's

nine little islands was represented: singers from each community performing three or four songs – some of welcome, others of island legends, others versifying modern events like World War II battles, and the Apollo moon missions.

The Queen and Duke left by the same route and in the same manner as they had come. Only the warm, saturating rain and the noticeable, underlying sadness of departure distinguished the two events. Anticipating the rain, the Queen had her transparent umbrella ready, but her hosts had provided a much more colourful substitute.

"Tuvalu," the Prime Minister had told the Queen, "has little in the way of land or natural resources, but we believe we have a happiness, culture and friendliness which are perhaps more important than pure material wealth." No-one who spent those two days on Funafuti could possibly doubt the truth of the assertion. Those qualities were evident everywhere and always, making Tuvalu one country at least that the Queen must have been genuinely sorry to leave.

attempt to outshine her hosts, she chose a subdued yet elegant cerise evening dress with just a fraction of the sparkle sported by the Pearly folk and showed that, within sight of her 81st birthday and despite, as she herself admits, "failing in sight and limbs," she can still command respect as one of the most poised members of the Royal Family.

The Pearlies, quintessential representatives of the Cockneys whose affection for the Royal Family is well known, presented Princess Alice not only with a

Like her son and daughter-in-law, Princess Alice Duchess of Gloucester is a regular visitor to major farming exhibitions, and her presence on 6th July at the Royal Show at Stoneleigh (above and top) was the continuation of a practice which is perhaps almost taken for granted. After a two-month summer break, Princess Alice's official diary began in earnest with a visit to County Hall in London to attend the Pearly Kings' and Queens' annual charity ball on 1st October (opposite page). Eschewing flamboyance herself, and in any event wisely deciding not to

bouquet of freesias and asters (opposite page, centre) but also with a Pearly doll (opposite page, bottom right) which has no doubt found its way into the hands of one or both of her grand-daughters, Lady Davina and Lady Rose Windsor.

Her second engagement of the autumn, on 11th October, involved a short trip from her London home at Kensington Palace to the Royal Albert Hall, to watch a gala of Gilbert and Sullivan operas – where else to meet the Yeoman of the Guard? (right) – presented by Solid Rock Foundation in aid of the Mental Health Foundation and the

D'Oyly Carte Opera Trust. Princess Alice was at this time putting the finishing touches to her memoirs, but in the meantime one of her former butlers, Peter Russell, had published his own highly entertaining – if on the face of it a trifle far-fetched – anecdotal memoirs, *Butler Royal*. They confirmed the generally held view that the late Duke had a temper worthy of any military man, but that Princess Alice soon learned how to draw upon her reserves of resourcefulness and determination to circumvent it.

When you are a major fashion show's guest of honour among 600 connoisseurs of Western chic, your entrance has to be spectacular. So on 9th November, while the Prince of Wales was tramping his estates in Cornwall, his wife put on her latest and most fetching evening dress for her visit to the Guildhall in London, where the charity Birthright was able to raise £30,000 gross towards funds for their research into the problems of childbirth. Preceded by a dinner, the show, organized by the Princess'

fashion advisor Anna Harvey, consisted of over a hundred British, and a few additional French designs, from the ultimate in gold-embroidered silk ball gowns to the less subtle allurements of plastic-boned bodices. Many of the Princess' own favourite designers were among the exhibitors. Unfortunately, Diana's slim look rebounded on her. Within a week she was widely and persistently rumoured to have contracted anorexia nervosa, the slimmers' disease which can cause death. Aware that her sister, Lady Sarah McCorquodale was once a victim, and that the disease is hereditary, a public genuinely anxious about the extremes to which the Princess appeared to be going to regain her shape after Prince William's birth was fed graphic newspaper accounts of her supposed decline. Palace denials did not convince many – and still have not – that she was at that time enjoying normal health.

called Valentine, to add to her already impressive possessions at the royal stables (left). Prince Claus' illness forced him to miss some engagements, but it was a smiling farewell for all on 19th November (right).

Eight members of the Royal Family were at Westminster Pier on 16th November to welcome Queen Beatrix and Prince Claus of the Netherlands for a four-day State visit. The visitors' arrival followed a trip in the ceremonial barge *Royal Nore* from Greenwich, where they were met by the Prince of Wales. In the customary exchange of gifts, Queen Elizabeth received a horse

After the explosion of reportage on the subject of Prince Andrew's exploits with the actress Koo Stark, it was inevitable that he should be idolised by a crowd of young girls on one of his rare public engagements. On 18th November, he was invited to switch on the Christmas lights in Regent Street. The rush to see the Prince gave the police a difficult job, but female screams were hushed long enough for him to complete the ceremony and say a few words. He referred to the long-held belief that Christmas trees – the theme of the illuminations – were introduced into England by the Prince Consort, and as he threw the switch he said, "I'm told there are 55,000 bulbs in those Christmas trees. I just hope they all work." Give or take one or two, they did and the Prince then attended a reception (these pages) given by the Regent Street Association.

Rarely do the Prince and Princess of Wales miss an opportunity to assist with fund-raising for the Mountbatten Memorial Trust, and the European premiere of *Gandhi,* held amid enormous publicity at the Odeon Theatre in London's Leicester Square, was a case in point. Countess Mountbatten was there, as was Barbara Cartland, together with a galaxy of international film celebrities, and those directly connected with the film – Sir Richard Attenborough, Sir John Gielgud, Sir John Mills and Ben Kingsley. The Prince and Princess' entrance was impressive, the Princess re-calling one of the most elegant gowns of her 1981 wardrobe. Prince Charles was

quietly satisfied with all he saw and heard, as everyone craned their necks for a glimpse of his glittering wife. She suffered from the intense heat of the brilliant television lights – "If you stand here long enough, you nearly pass out," she said during another premiere six months later. And this occasion failed to pass without a reference to Prince William. "He never stops eating," the Princess told Sir John Mills.

sunlit morning of 6th December he joined the Quorn hunt for a chase over the snow covered countryside near Melton Mowbray in Leicestershire. The outing – the Prince was unaccompanied by his wife – did nothing to stem yet another newspaper report that their sixteen-month-old marriage was in difficulties. The *Daily Mail's* gossip columnist, Nigel Dempster, added fuel to that particular fire when, in an interview on American television, he branded the Princess of Wales a "fiend" who "is very much ruling the roost" and making Prince Charles "desperately unhappy". In Britain, Dempster refused to withdraw, on the grounds that if the Princess was "making the Prince unhappy, we should know about it." Buckingham Palace condemned the comments as "totally stupid" and revealed that the Princess was "very upset" by them.

Like Princess Anne, the Prince of Wales has become a devotee of fox hunting, and has attracted his fair share of critics for doing so. They failed to dissuade him when, on the crisp,

Barbican Theatre. The choice of play was no coincidence. Almost fifty years before, its author J. M. Barrie bequeathed the royalties from his book to the Great Ormond Street Hospital. Now under severe financial strictures, the hospital was grateful for the capital asset and royal support.

The Great Ormond Street Hospital for Sick Children made the most of its royal patronage in December. On the 2nd, the Princess of Wales visited the hospital amid a great show of popularity from nursing and administration staff. On 15th December, the Queen, who is the hospital's patron, attended a performance (these pages) of the Royal Shakespeare Company's new production of *Peter Pan* at the

With the approach of Christmas, the inevitable party season got under way, and the Royal Family were not left out. On 16th December Princess Michael of Kent went to East London to attend a Christmas party at Wanstead Almshouses (bottom left). A week beforehand her brother-in-law the Duke of Kent attended a Variety Club lunch with a particularly Christmas flavour about it. Staged at the London Hilton Hotel, the lunch marked the end of the Club's Christmas toy campaign in which 20,000 toys were distributed to

sick and deprived children throughout the country. It also featured the Variety Club's famous "Miss Christmases", drawn from the casts of musicals *Song and Dance* and *Cats*: they are seen (top right) with the Duke at the pre-lunch reception. After the lunch, the Duke received a cheque for the RNLI, of which he is President, and which saved no fewer that 1,281 lives at sea in 1982.

The Duchess of Kent, meanwhile, kept a regular annual Christmas appointment by attending the Not Forgotten Association's Christmas party, held at the Royal Riding Stables at Buckingham Palace (pictures above). Publicity tends to be concentrated on the Association's older members, particularly the Chelsea Pensioners, but recent campaigns continue to result in many younger men and women benefiting from its efforts. The MP Hugh Rossi told an audience of 350 at the party that there were now over a quarter of a million disabled war pensioners, with ages ranging from 25 to over 100.

One of the oldest, 101-year-old

courage it can inspire made her encounter with fourteen children a moving experience. She was there to present the annual Children of Courage Awards (above, below and left), and to make the acquaintance of children who had overcome cancer, bone disease, brain damage and blindness to live active, useful lives. Others had performed mountain rescues, chased burglars and saved friends from collapsing masonry. Their citations were read out during the presentation ceremony, and the Queen Mother gave each an award – in the shape of a bird set in perspex – and a citation scroll. Then, in front of a Christmas tree in the Deanery Courtyard, they all posed with her for a photograph to commemorate a pleasant finale to an exciting year.

Frederick Page, who served in Persia and lost an eye at the Dardenelles, shared the ceremonial knife with the Duchess of Kent as this year's cake was cut. Baked by the Army Catering Corps, the cake was iced with a replica of the Association's badge. Like that in the Duchess' left lapel, it showed the head of an elephant. As Patron of the Spastics Society, the Duchess was present two days later (left) at the International Show Jumping Championships at Olympia in aid of the Stars' Association for Spastics.

The catalogue of misfortune calling the Queen Mother to Westminster Abbey on 15th December is hardly the stuff of which Christmas is made, but the

Prince William (previous pages), was among four royal infants absent from Christmas Day mattins at St George's Chapel. But, excepting Prince Edward and the Queen Mother, everyone else attended. Less familiar faces included Captain Phillips with son Peter (right) and the Kent children Nicholas, Helen and George talking to Viscount Linley and his sister Sarah (bottom right).

RAF Benson has received many royal visitors; the Queen's Flight, established by King Edward VIII in 1936 at Hendon, has been based there continuously for 37 years, and Prince Edward gained his glider's wings there in 1980. On 12th January Princess Alexandra – equal first with the Duke of Gloucester for performing the first royal public engagement of 1983 – paid a four-hour visit to the base. Elegantly and well wrapped up against a bleak winter's day, her first job was to join the officers of the Queen's Flight for a group photograph (below). A forty-minute inspection of the Queen's Flight followed, before the Princess was taken to the sergeants' mess for a reception at which she signed the visitors' book. Luncheon at the officers' mess was taken to the

accompaniment of a selection of waltzes and film themes played by the Salon Orchestra of the Central Band of the RAF. During the afternoon, the Princess toured the station's twelve-roomed sports pavilion, and the education section where she met some of the families of RAF

personnel at an informal, hour-long tea party.
(Above and top) Princess Alexandra, who is patron of the English National Opera Company, visited its rehearsal and production centre at Lilian Baylis House in Hampstead on 25th January.

Royalty from Britain and Spain met on 13th January when a tercentenary exhibition of paintings by the Spanish artist Murillo opened at the Royal Academy of Arts in London. The Duke and Duchess of Gloucester (below) arrived first, five minutes before Queen Sophie of Spain.

The Royal Academy of Arts again entertained royalty when the Prince and Princess of Wales attended a reception (left) in connection with "Britain Salutes New York" – a festival marking the bicentenary of the end of the American War of Independence. This was the Prince and Princess' first official engagement since their short but eventful, far-from-private holiday in Liechtenstein as guests of that principality's heir apparent Prince Hans Adam. Prince Charles and his wife rarely had a chance to avoid the attentions of photographers, both British and continental, and the entire holiday of just less than a week was ruined by cat-and-mouse tactics. After

some pretty harsh words from the Prince's detective, the British press cried off, but the foreign contingent was not so easily deterred. In the event it was surprising that the royal couple were in a mood to smile at all when they got back to London. The Duke of Kent was luckier. He went off on 20th January to Sestriere in Northern Italy to attend the Kandahar/Martini International Ski-ing Championships, and was able to find time to keep up his ski-ing practice in between attending receptions and awarding prizes during the five-day event (remaining pictures). Unlike January 1982 at Meribel, in France, his family did not accompany him.

It was a little late for Valentine's Day, but as it was just over two years to the day since her engagement, the Princess of Wales might have thought the heart-shaped bouquet (above) appropriate as she began her visit to Brookfields School for Mentally Handicapped Children at Tilehurst on 25th February. "She's a natural," was the most often repeated compliment. "I'd have her on my staff any day," added the school's headmaster.

western hemisphere she has ever undertaken. The royal couple arrived at Kingston, Jamaica (top left) in scorching weather which made sub-zero Britain seem light years away. The welcoming procedures (far left) were as standard as the following day's cultural "Salute to the Queen" was typically Jamaican. Scores

Just over three months after landing in London from a month-long tour of Australia and the South Pacific, the Queen left Heathrow Airport with Prince Philip on 13th February for the most extensive tour of the

Alexander Bustamente, preceded a medley of traditional folk tunes in celebration of Jamaica's twenty first year of independence. The Queen, showed genuine pleasure (left) at this

of thousands of almost uncontrollable Jamaicans forgot their everyday problems and put on their finest show of sometimes almost delirious enthusiasm (top and far right). An imaginative parade of fifteen historical effigies, from Christopher Columbus to Jamaica's first president, Sir

colourful show. "Every time Prince Philip and I come here," she told the Governor-General at a State banquet that evening, "you seem to have some special event to greet us."
Earlier that day she had been to Gordon House to address the Jamaican Parliament. She praised the country's

maintenance of democratic principles despite what she termed "pressures and strains that have stretched its social fabric" – a reference to a period of tumultuous and bloody unrest at the time of the 1980 elections, in which the former left-wing premier Michael Manley was defeated. His aspirations

to turn the country into a republic were thought to have been effectively put in their place by the Queen's reference to herself as "Queen of Jamaica," but in fact this is her common practice in all countries acknowledging her as sovereign. A walkabout afterwards (bottom right) showed she certainly enjoyed great popular support.

On 15th February the Queen and Duke visited Montego Bay, and saw twelve thousand people packed into Sam Sharpe Square as she attended a civic reception (below) and watched a march past (opposite page).

Plans for the Queen to sail in *Britannia* to Santa Barbara on 1st March were scuppered by storms which put the city's harbour out of action, and she and Prince Philip had to fly from Long Beach to rejoin the Reagans, who were by now beginning to feel personally apologetic for the continuing bad weather. Their arrival was attended by all the hastily-prepared ritual of State – there followed a hazardous twenty-mile journey by car through the flooded roads winding up to the Reagan's 700-acre ranch in the Santa Ynez mountains.

The plans at the Reagan ranch fizzled out equally effectively. There was lunch of course, but the invitation to go riding – a reciprocal gesture for the amicable episode at Windsor nine months before – had to be called off in favour of a simple photo-call (left and right) for which neither hosts nor guests seemed to have much enthusiasm. There was no let up in the chaos caused by worsening rain during the following few days. Things reached an all time low when the Queen and Prince Philip were forced to book into a hotel in San Francisco on the night of 2nd March, instead of spending that night on board *Britannia*. But the following evening all seemed forgiven at the State dinner given by President Reagan at the de Young Memorial Museum. "I knew before we came," mused the Queen (below), "that we had exported many of our traditions to the United States. I had not realised that the weather was one of them."

Bristol Hospital for Sick Children's intensive care unit (above, left and below) but only the young patients enjoyed her company as she sat on their beds, watched them at play, and told them not to suck thumbs. And after visiting wards where children were suffering from cancer and leukemia, she was told by one her hosts, "I have never seen anyone establish a rapport with patients in the way you have." A month later, on 2nd March, she opened a £7 million shopping precinct in Aylesbury (opposite page and pictures far left) and was highly amused to discover a cosmetic called Starkers. "I didn't know they made nude make-up," she said.

The combination of the Princess of Wales and children in hospital brings out the best in both. On 4th February, two thousand people saw her open the

There were no surprise royal visitors, and no surprise absentees, at the Badminton Horse Trials from 14th to 17th April. The Queen gave the event the prestige it habitually derives from her presence, much to the evident satisfaction of the Duke of Beaufort (below) who celebrated his 83rd birthday ten days beforehand. Prince and

Princess Michael (far left),
active participants in hunting
and point-to-points, attended
again and the royal Phillipses
were represented in full.
Princess Anne, still trying
desparately to bring on two
young horses for eventing
herself, watched the proceedings
and carried her two-year-old
daughter Zara around in between
times, stopping for a quick look
at a pair of draught horses
(opposite page, top right).
With them was five-year-old
Peter, now in his second year at

Minchinhampton Blue Boys School. Lying sixth after the dressage – only 6.6 points behind the leader Mike Tucker of Dalwhinnie, Captain Phillips was forced to retire when his horse Classic Lines refused at the eleventh fence in the cross country, and threw its rider to the ground.

In a thrilling finish, it was Lucinda Green on Regal Realm who won for the fifth time. The Queen presented the Whitbread Trophy with the warm congratulations of a woman who appreciates good horsemanship. And, as usual (these pages), she was back on the Badminton estate on Sunday 17th April to attend the customary church service. She is seen (above) leaving Badminton House with the Duke of Beaufort, Prince Philip and Princess Anne that morning.

The army had its share of royal favour during the year, too, and the Queen Mother was a frequent guest of honour. On 10th May she arrived at Colchester to visit the Royal Anglian Regiment. The weather proved less welcoming than her hosts: as she began her inspection of

the six guards of honour, a sudden downpour caught everyone unawares. She happily continued her inspection (top left) before watching a parade (left) and touring the Meeanee and Hyderabad Barracks (above and opposite page, bottom right). Security was tight on this occasion, but not nearly so stringent as for her visit to celebrate the 75th anniversary of the Territorial Army in Northern Ireland six weeks later. Then, the Queen Mother – who could well have justified staying at home – showed both personal courage and a confidence in the arrangements being made for her safety. A rash of bomb scares failed to deter her. Far from it: she fairly ambled through her schedule as if she were in the familiar surroundings of her own back garden. In so doing, she honoured her hosts, encouraged the local community and won for herself universal praise for putting duty first.

The Princess of Wales oozed confidence during her first public outing since returning from Australasia with Prince Charles. After her resounding success down-under, she was out doing her favourite thing, making friends with the young. It was 13th May, and the

Princess visited two centres for handicapped children – the Gloucestershire Adventure Playground at Coberley – where she picked up and cuddled five-year-old Andrew Harrison, who ran towards her with great excitement – and Paradise House College at Painswick.

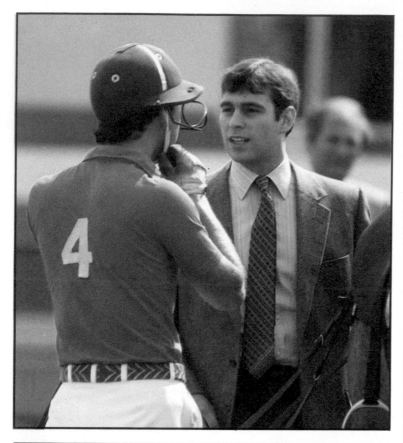

becomes almost newsworthy. Prince Andrew was at Smith's Lawn Windsor on 15th May to watch Prince Charles play in his first match since returning from Australasia, where he played three times and was on the winning side each time. Also present at Windsor were Lord and Lady Tryon, once fast friends of Prince Charles.

Prince Andrew, due to carry out solo engagements during his time in Britain that summer, was allotted a private secretary, Squadron Leader Adam Wise, formerly the Queen's equerry, from the beginning of October.

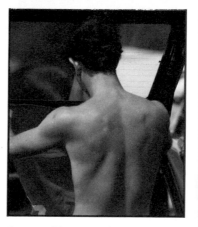

A spot of innocent horse-play never comes amiss, especially on the polo field, and when it develops between a couple of fun-loving brothers who happen to be first and third in succession to the Throne, it

One event Princess Margaret rarely misses each year is the Royal Caledonian Ball, held on 16th May at the Grosvenor House Hotel. A month previously, a new biography of the Princess – written by Christopher Warwick, who has admired her for many years – appeared very much as the Princess' own account of some of the controversies of her eventful and sometimes stormy life.

Prince Charles won a medal; his team Maple Leaf won a cup (below left); but the Princess of Wales won everybody's attention with her casual, stylish pedal-pushers, when she arrived at Smith's Lawn on 25th May. With sunglasses perched on her blow-away hair, she looked thoroughly relaxed, watching her husband's team beat Saracens.

The Queen had, perhaps, less to
smile about at the Epsom Derby
on 1st June (following pages).
Her colt Special Leave had been
withdrawn after an indifferent
trials performance, and victory
passed to the hands of others.
But the presence of Prince
Philip, Princess Anne, the Queen
Mother and the Duke and Duchess
of Gloucester made it a relaxing
family event.

Towards the end of April it was announced that the Queen had appointed three more Knights of the Most Noble Order of the Garter. These were the Duke of Norfolk, hereditary Earl Marshal of England, Admiral of the Fleet Lord Lewin and Lord Richardson of Duntisbourne. On 13th June, the Throne Room at Windsor Castle was filled with almost the entire complement of Knights as the new boys were installed at the annual chapter. After the customary lunch, the service of the Order was held in St George's Chapel, the Queen, Prince Philip, the Prince of Wales and the Queen Mother bringing up the rear of the impressive, slow-moving procession (overleaf).

The Royal Family was out in force again for the four days of Royal Ascot (following pages) from 14th to 17th June, bringing a touch of level-headedness to a meeting frenzied with preoccupation about hairstyles and dress lengths. The big fad this year was the coiffing of hair into effective hats – one head of long hair was teased up and lacquered to form a top hat; another was ranged radially to form a Japanese parasol. Mrs Gertrude Shilling caught the Queen's eye – but necessarily only fleetingly – with a messy turmoil of Union Jacks bearing the motto "Buy British" while a German designer, Besant by name, sported a hat comprising nothing but mirrors, explaining that "when the sun comes out it sparkles."

The nearest any member of the Royal Family got to extravagant styles was the cartwheel-brimmed hat which the Duchess of Gloucester wore on the first day. For the rest, it was noticed that the absent Princess of Wales' predilection for boaters had taken the Queen's fancy, and that pill-boxes were as popular with Princess Anne as ever. Pleasant though it was, the occasion may not prove particularly memorable for the Queen. She had not a single runner in the entire four-day programme, and the BBC's live broadcasting blackout deprived her of a television commentary in the royal box. The Queen Mother asked the BBC's racing correspondent whether he couldn't do his commentary on Ascot's closed circuit TV instead. "That was nice of her," he beamed.

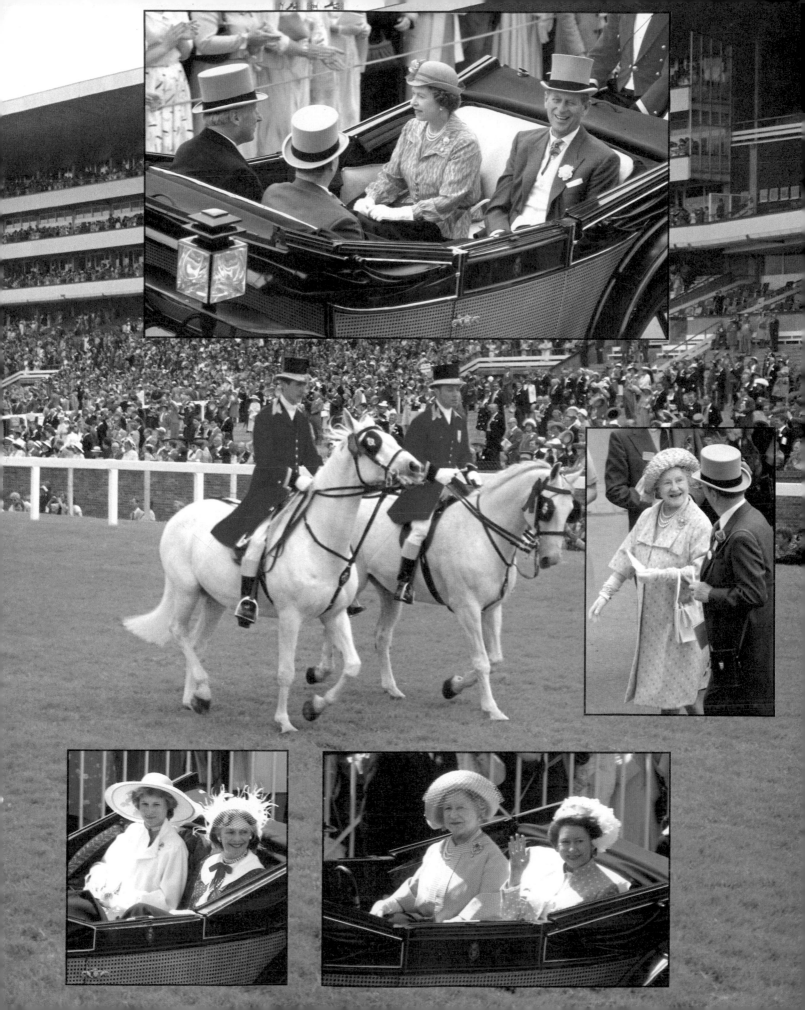

Mid-1983 was a particularly happy time for Prince and Princess Michael of Kent as they emerged from Westminster Cathedral at the end of July (left and below), their five-year-old marriage finally recognised and blessed by the Roman Catholic Church. The Prince and Princess attend Anglican and Catholic church services on alternate Sundays. The Queen was all smiles, too, when opening the Royal Society of Edinburgh's premises (below left), and holding a garden party at Holyroodhouse (right) on 29th June. The following day, she reviewed the Royal Scots Regiment there (opposite, below), with Princess Anne (bottom left). The Princess attended many of the regiment's celebrations in this, its 350th year, including an anniversary ball at Edinburgh's Assembly Rooms (below, far left).

Prince Andrew's visit to Newport, Rhode Island in mid-July, in support of Britain's America's Cup challenge, began with a reception at the Old Colony House. Smiles hid his concern as IRA protestors heckled his arrival. The crackle of a gun salute made him and his detective jump, before both realised their mistake and were convulsed with relieved laughter. The Prince was in Rhode Island as guest of Peter de Savary, whose efforts to secure the America's Cup for Britain were expensive, unsparing and, in the unhappy event, unsuccessful. The Cup went to Australia, though all that happened long after Prince Andrew had enjoyed an active and exciting trip.

It was only to be expected of a man about to embark on his fifth year in the Royal Navy that Prince Andrew found himself thoroughly at home on the motor launch *Lisanola,* from which he saw Britain's

Victory '83 being put through her paces during one of many practice runs. He had the good fortune to be invited aboard the yacht, and tried his hand at sailing her.

Relishing the traditional delights of August's Cowes Week, Prince Philip looked relaxed and in good humour, piloting *Yeoman XXI* (left), or snatching a moment's earnest conversation with his royal cousin and crew member, King Constantine of Greece (top). The King's teenage daughter, Princess Alexia was also there (right) as was Prince Edward, who attended both as learner (above) and as competitor.

If the Queen Mother's birthday doesn't quite have`the status which offers her daughter the full ceremonial of Trooping the Colour, it is nevertheless an established part of the summer season. Even its ritual is becoming familiar: the assembly of a crowd of hundreds outside the doors of Clarence House, and the chorus of cheers and applause as a large-brimmed hat, bobbing into sight on an upper terrace, eventually reveals a beaming birthday girl (right), bright as a button, proud as Punch, half amused, half moved by the admiring audience below. The odd toddler (bottom picture) hogs the attention for a while – a small distraction compared with what follows

when the Queen Mother comes down to greet her well-wishers. In a reassuring breach of the generation gap, the braver children storm an unobtrusive police guard, and the luckier or more persistent ones reach their royal target with a volley of flowers, cards and chocolates (left, below left). The less fortunate (bottom) find the London bobby a willing intermediary. On this pleasant August morning, the crowds were rewarded by the sight of the Queen Mother's two daughters (below) and the Prince and Princess of Wales enjoying this informal atmosphere before the celebrant's final wave (right).

After a fortnight spent going separate ways, there was a royal reunion on 14th August, when the Queen led her family off *Britannia*'s barge to meet the Queen Mother at Scrabster. Prince Andrew sported a new and, in events, brief beard, while Princess Anne, on the eve of her 33rd birthday, carried her $2\frac{1}{2}$-

year-old daughter Zara ashore (right). The Queen Mother had travelled from the Castle of Mey, where the previous day she had attended a local horticultural show (left). The family came together again for the Braemar Games (above) early in September. As usual, the Prince and Princess of Wales, Princess Alexandra and Mr Angus Ogilvy joined the royal party.

Prince Charles, Princess Diana and Prince William made their own way to their Balmoral holiday, but even royal vacations are fragmented, and both the Prince and Princess undertook several official engagements from the Castle that summer. Princess Diana's brief, private visit to London fired new speculation, which took two months to subside, that she was pregnant, while 14-month-old Prince William contributed to the family's holiday excitement by escaping his nanny's attention and setting off the security alarms. Detectives within the Castle, and police squads without, were quick to react, if rather slower to appreciate the funny side.

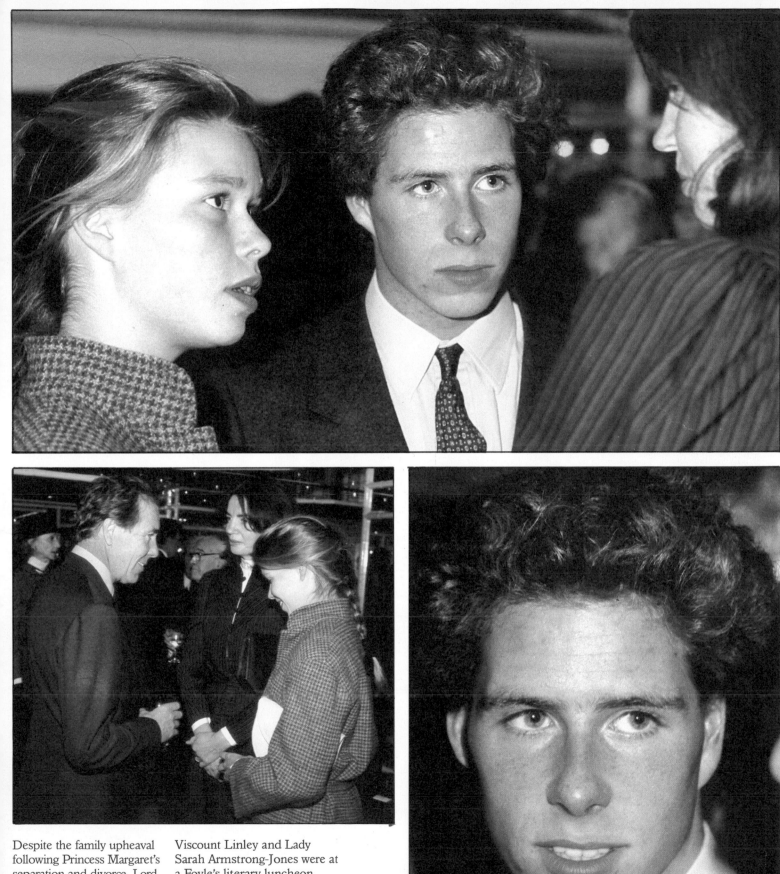

Despite the family upheaval following Princess Margaret's separation and divorce, Lord Snowdon's relationship with their children remained firm and cordial. Witness the event in October 1983, when

Viscount Linley and Lady Sarah Armstrong-Jones were at a Foyle's literary luncheon in London to help their father and stepmother (above) launch Lord Snowdon's new photographic book, *Sittings*.

Memories dominated early November. On the 2nd, the Queen unveiled Lord Mountbatten's statue at Horse Guards (top) before almost all the Royal Family (above, far left). The following week, the Queen Mother (opposite) again visited the Field of Remembrance at Westminster, and joined many relatives at the Cenotaph on Remembrance Day. On this occasion it was Prince Charles who laid the first wreath, rather than the Queen, who was then in Kenya.

Kenya's Remembrance Day was observed on the original Armistice anniversary, 11th November, and the Queen and Prince Philip led Kenya's and the Commonwealth's tribute in a quiet, solemn ceremony in Nairobi. Her cluster of poppies and the black of her gloves, shoes and patterned dress offered the only similarities to the sombre garb of a Whitehall ceremony: Prince Philip's tropical rig looked strangely incongruous. This was not the only wreath the Queen laid that day: early in the morning she had placed a tribute of white lilies on the tomb of Jomo Kenyatta, the former President who had led his country to independence in 1963.

Buffalo at close range (right) failed to deter the Queen as, with marksman Richard Prickett (above) she toured the Treetops water hole where, almost 32 years before, she succeeded to the Throne. Both the Queen and the Prince seemed bemused by the drastic changes they saw.

Her grandfather, King George V attended his Durbar here in 1911; her uncle was installed as Viceroy in 1947; her father was the country's last King-Emperor; and after twenty-three years the Queen herself was back in Delhi. In 1961 she had been greeted by President Nehru. Now his daughter, Mrs Indira Gandhi welcomed Her Majesty, who looked delighted to be visiting India again.

The massive, Lutyens-designed Hyderabad House, with its reminders of the British Raj, was the setting for some informal talks between the Queen and Mrs Ghandi, which were filmed for inclusion in the Queen's Christmas message a month later.

The Queen visited the fabled Red Fort in Delhi (left) and Mahatma Gandhi's tomb at Rajghat. Here she wore, in place of her own shoes, airline 'slipperettes'. (Above and right) a pre-lunch photo-call with Mrs Gandhi at Hyderabad House. (Opposite, below) the Queen presenting the Order of Merit to Mother Theresa in Delhi the following day.

Highlight of the Queen's second day in India was her tour of St Thomas' School. Greeted by girls with incense trays (above), she visited the primary department (right) and then hopped into a palanquin carried by senior girls – dressed as male bearers – who performed a play called *The Awakening of Indian Womanhood*.

(Previous pages) the Princess of Wales at Wantage on 2nd December (right) and visiting victims of the Harrods bomb explosion on the 19th. The approach of Prince William's second Christmas was marked by a photo session in the garden of his parents' London home, Kensington Palace.

Crown-Princess Marie-Aglae of Liechtenstein (left) accompanied the Prince and Princess of Wales on the Alpine slopes at the start of their skiing holiday on 8th January, 1984. The early bargain struck between Prince

and Press was honoured and the royal couple eventually soared to the top of Hoch Eck (right and bottom) to begin a much appreciated private vacation.

A succession of royal gala evenings brightened a gloomy British winter. On 23rd February, the Queen Mother attended the Elgar commemorative concert at Westminster Abbey (far left). She was at the Odeon, Leicester Square, for the premiere of *Champions* eight days later (left), with Princess Anne (opposite, top centre). The Queen also visited the Odeon (opposite, top left) to see *The Dresser* on 19th March. On 12th April, the Duchess of Kent attended the Amir of Bahrain's State banquet in London (opposite, top right), while a month earlier, Prince and Princess Michael (this page) had attended a London Coliseum performance of the opera *Gloriana*. The Princess exuded that special combination of regality and informal charm that has earned her the description "More royal than the royals".

The Queen and Prince Philip left London on 23rd March for a five-day State Visit to Jordan. Controversial for its political and security implications, the tour began cautiously, with a stop-over in Cyprus and a circuitous route avoiding Syria. But it was all smiles when the royal couple finally arrived (these pages) in Amman to be greeted by King Hussein, whose

sometimes precarious political relations with the West have never shaken his personal friendship with the British Royal Family. His regard for the Queen and Prince Philip was reflected in the resplendent banquet he and Queen Noor (far left) gave that first evening – a full State occasion, with every royal utterance scrupulously combed for political undertones. The Queen praised King Hussein's unceasing attempts to find a solution to the Palestinian problem, while the King addressed his country's cause to the 'sense of justice of the British people. We appreciate their courageous views and keenness to eliminate the mistakes of the past.'

Everything and everyone was dwarfed by the dimensions of Petra, the ancient trading centre built by the Nabateans two thousand years ago. The Queen and Prince Philip, accompanied as they were almost everywhere on this tour by Hussein and his Queen, walked into the ruined city to capture the grandeur of its approaches.

Petra was heavily guarded (above) and cleared of most of its cave-dwelling families, though some inhabitants – including this New Zealand-born mother (top) – were presented to the Queen. This was her last sightseeing event of the tour, and the royal couple stayed at King Hussein's palace at Aqaba that night, leaving (left) next day.

Princess Diana admitted the effects of morning sickness at Leicester in March (above), but at Stanmore the next day (right), seemed in good spirits. With the approach of Easter, no end of presents were being offered her – a knitted doll for her baby at Glastonbury (top right) and Easter eggs for Prince William at Stoke (left).

For the first time in 172 years women officers took part in the Sovereign's Parade at Sandhurst, where the Duchess of Kent took the Salute on 6th April. Just after the Queen's Jordanian visit, Queen Noor (above right) saw her nephew receive his commission.

With the Duke of Beaufort's death only two months before, Badminton Horse Trials in April inevitably lacked its usual festive air. But the Queen was there (far right), and Captain Mark Phillips (left) competed, though unsuccessfully, while his children Peter (right) and Zara (above) looked as mischievous as ever, and provided the public with some entertaining distractions.

Spring flowers for the Princess of Wales as she arrived at Wellington College at Crowthorne on 16th April, to hear the National Children's Orchestra in rehearsal. Though she is patron of the orchestra, she admitted that music was not her strong point at school. Prince William might do better, however, as his mother was presented with a quarter-size violin to take back for him. Next day, Princess Alexandra was presenting radio and television awards in London – to the delight of the BBC who bagged most of them. Jan Leeming, Frank Bough and David Coleman (opposite page) were proud recipients, while ITV's George Cole and Dennis Waterman (bottom left) made the most of their moment of glory.

The Queen discharged her annual Maundy obligations this year at one of the most attractive of small English cathedrals, when she distributed purses of specially-minted money to 58 men and 58 women at Southwell Minster, near Newark, on 19th April. Then she and Prince

Philip met ice-dancing royalty when Olympic champions Jayne Torvill and Christopher Dean were presented at a Nottingham Council reception. After the enormous surge of patriotism and pride which surrounded the young couple as they easily secured their gold medal at Sarajevo – an achievement watched by Princess Anne and on which the Queen personally telegraphed her congratulations – this was a most popular royal event.

Seemingly incapable of radiating anything but the joy of being an octogenarian, the doyenne of the Royal Family was as busy as ever on 10th May, 1984. That afternoon, the Queen Mother went to All Saints Church at Ascot to open its new church hall (these pages). She has no particular connection with the church, but that didn't stop her from enjoying a pleasantly informal afternoon, brightened by the singing of its forty-strong choir. Of course, they asked her to pose for a photograph, and the Queen Mother obliged, as she always does. And as she's also good at planting trees, she did that too.

A selection of Prince Charles' early season polo matches. (Above) playing at Windsor on 13th May for Ingwenya against Downey Fields in the final of the Rodney Moore Cup: Ingwenya won 4-2. (Left and top right) on the same day, playing for Windsor against Travelwise: Windsor lost 9-6½. (Opposite page, top left and top right) playing at Windsor on 19th May for Rajasthan Polo Club against Laurent Perrier. The Queen saw his team lose 7-3. (Right and far left) playing at Windsor on 24th May for Les Diables Bleus, beating Chopendoz 8-7 in front of the Princess of Wales. (Far right, and opposite, top centre) in the quarter finals of the Queen's Cup at Windsor on 3rd June, when his team, Les Diables Bleus, beat Piaget 10-7.

By most accounts the Royal Windsor Horse Show lacked the touch of extravagance usually associated with this prestigious annual event, but any occasion staged at Home Park, Windsor, within sight of the Queen's Berkshire home, and graced by royalty determined to enjoy their day's leisure, cannot be mediocre for long. So even the threat of indifferent weather could not put off the many spectators as the Queen sported her most comfortable, functional country clothes to tramp the ground where Prince Philip would be competing during the four-day event. As is often the case, the Duke's only surviving sister, Princess Sophie of Hanover (bottom left) belied her 70 years to brave a cold, breezy day in support of her brother, whose two-fold aim was to regain the Harrods International Driving Grand

Prix which he lost last year, and win a place in the British team for the World Driving Championships in Hungary in August. Princess Anne (above), Prince Edward and Prince Paul of Greece (top picture) were there to see Prince Philip take the lead after the first day's presentation and dressage (opposite page), despite a strict line taken by the judges, and a heart stopping

moment when his two leading horses suddenly took a dislike to each other. Prince Philip, who had suffered a number of spills earlier in the season when driving novice horses, seemed much more confident after his near victory the previous week at a Brighton carriage-driving event (in which Prince Michael also competed), and was in any case back with his familiar team of Cleveland bays/Oldenburg crosses, owned by the Queen. These days, it seems, no major equestrian event escapes the presence of Princess Anne's two children, and sure enough, Master Peter Phillips looked engrossed with the proceedings as, supervised by the Queen (opposite page), he put his pair of miniature binoculars to good use. But his quiet

behaviour didn't last and, before long, he was being firmly taken in hand by Princess Anne (above). Sister Zara seemed much more amenable, possibly because she was looking forward to her 3rd birthday for which, four days later, she would throw a small party for her young friends and relations. There was also an unexpected treat at Windsor when Prince Philip allowed both Peter and Zara to ride in his driving carriage. Typically, it was Peter who took the whip, and commanded the horses, while Zara had to be reassured by her mother. Meanwhile, Prince

Philip had two more stages to complete, and unfortunately he was to lose ground. Going for total accuracy in the marathon lost him precious time points, and he was not helped by a broken carriage cable after colliding with a branch just before the obstacle section. In the final analysis, he had dropped to seventh place, and the Queen found herself once again congratulating Tjeerd Velstra, last year's winner, on retaining the championship. But she could afford a smile (top, with King Constantine): her own private carriage won a coaching event, and Prince Philip still secured his passage to Hungary.

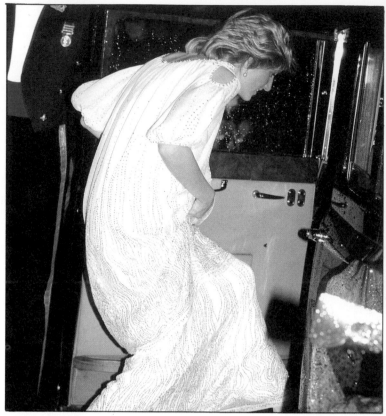

The Princess of Wales looking proudly pregnant (above) as she awaited her car after a banquet given by the President of the Royal Society of Arts, Sir Hugh Casson, (right) in Piccadilly on 14th May. Back in September, both the Princess and Sir Hugh had submitted their own portrait sketches of Prince William and Prince Charles respectively for a publication in aid of Mencap. The Princess wore white again, but this time with gold sequins, for the Royal Opera House Development Appeal concert six days later (top right and opposite).

Few royals can resist visiting the Chelsea Flower Show, held this year on 21st May. The Queen (above and opposite, top left) attended with Princess Margaret (right and far left), another regular visitor; the Duchess of Gloucester (above) accompanied Princess Alice; and Princess Michael (left)

may have picked up a few tips for her new rose garden at Nether Lyppiatt. Royal husbands included Prince Charles, who took Princess Diana along, and Prince Michael, though Prince Philip had to cry off at the last moment to attend World Wildlife Fund meetings in Washington.

Princess Michael looked every inch the Edwardian beauty in a classic, figure-hugging evening robe, and a choker which would have made even Queen Alexandra a trifle jealous. With Prince Michael, she was attending a gala performance at the London Coliseum on 22nd May of *Onegin*, by the late John Cranko, chosen by the London Festival Ballet to open its 1984 season.

(Top, and opposite page) a colourfully-dressed Princess Alexandra visiting Cranleigh School in Surrey on 23rd May, while on the same day the Princess of Wales was making her second visit to the Albany Trust in Deptford (left). She had to run the gauntlet of several political controversies, including a plea to help prevent the possible abolition of the GLC. She said she would speak to her father, before a crucial vote in the House of Lords. Two of Princess Anne's many engagements in May took her to RAF Lyneham (top left) on the 3rd, and to the Surrey County Show at Guildford on the 28th (above, left). But it was a quiet month for Princess Michael, seen (above) competing at the Amberley Horse Trials on 5th May.

The high-goal polo season brought Prince Charles to Windsor on 24th May. His team won 8-7, to the delight of Princess Diana, who now really seems to enjoy polo.

The Queen Mother began a three-day tour of the Channel Islands on 30th May. First port of call was Guernsey, which 'holds many happy memories for me, renewed through the living bonds which continue to link Guernsey and the Crown.' As everywhere in the islands, the Queen Mother, who first visited them with King George VI in the aftermath of liberation exactly thirty-nine years before, was a popular guest, and nowhere more so than on Sark, where the genteel way of island life seemed tailor-made for the Queen Mother's very individual style of carrying out her duties. She forsook the helicopter in which she had arrived (left) for a horse and carriage (above),

the traditional means of touring the island. That evening, the Royal Yacht *Britannia*, in which she had sailed to Guernsey, took her to Jersey, where she landed the next morning (far right). As on previous days, her engagement book was packed, but she smiled and chatted her way through the receptions, visits and those Channel Island specialities, the *vins d'honneur*. The Queen Mother has been known in years past to try her hand at snooker or billiards. When she visited the Maufant Youth Centre in Jersey, she graduated to the pool table (left), slamming in a ball to the delight of her hosts who had tactfully placed it where she could hardly miss! Such is the prerogative of Queens, as indeed a tour such as this is the prerogative of their subjects. Normally, at this time of year, the Queen

Mother does a round trip taking in the Cinque Ports, of which she is Lord Warden. But, with the D-Day anniversary close by, nothing could have been more appropriate as this all too rare return to what Churchill called 'our dear Channel Islands.'

A sixty-eight-man parachute drop (opposite, top) by soldiers who had fought in the Falklands provided a spectacular start to Prince Charles' visit on 5th June to Ranville in Normandy to commemorate D-Day with the Parachute Regiment. It was a day of pride for the veterans who marched past their Colonel-in-Chief (top) and of gratitude for the Prince, who laid a wreath where 2,500 servicemen lie buried in the town's military cemetery (above).

(Left) the Princess of Wales attended the premiere of *Indiana Jones and the Temple of Doom*, in Leicester Square on 11th June. Next day Prince William posed – though over a week early – for a photocall at Kensington Palace in celebration of his second birthday, 21st June. Mother, child and family came together again – on the parade ground (above) and on the Palace balcony (following pages) for Trooping the Colour on 16th June.

The Princess of Wales took delivery of a new Ford Escort convertible late in Spring, and drove it to Cirencester on 28th June to watch Prince Charles play in the Warwickshire Cup. His team won, though narrowly, while his wife attracted the interest of spectators by her bright blue culottes and her healthy tan. It was only three days to her 23rd birthday, which she spent at yet another polo match, and which was celebrated by many tributes to the enormous contribution she had made in three years to the popularity of the monarchy.

"Two months later than planned, but better late than never!" September 24th, 1984 at last saw the Queen and Prince Philip in Canada for the fifteenth time. On this occasion the welcoming province was New Brunswick, high on bicentennial celebrations, and Moncton received the royal visitors. The ceremony of welcome followed a familiar pattern, but the unofficial antics of youngsters (above and right) lent a delightful unpredictability to it all. Julie McLean was there officially (opposite), and presented her bouquet beautifully.

Sunshine greeted the next day too, and leafy, loyalist Fredericton looked its pristine, sparkling best. The clash of bells drifting over its elegant streets called the faithful to prayer at Christ Church Cathedral, where two very special worshippers would head the congregation. Archbishop Nutter (far left) did the honours and, only ten days from the event, could not resist a congratulatory word to the Queen on the birth of Prince Harry. "I may say as a grandparent — and we have many grandparents in this congregation — how much we rejoice," he enthused. There was no whisper of dissent in the entire town — a reminder that loyalty and devotion to the Crown and those who represent it is almost a way of life here.

The Hotel Beauséjour was the Queen's home during her two-day stay at Moncton, but it also became a venue of State when, at the end of her second day, she and Prince Philip attended a banquet given by New Brunswick's Premier, Richard Hatfield. The Queen, resplendent in her gorgeous family jewels and wearing the Sovereign's insignia of the Order of Canada, made no secret of her pleasure at being back. "This is an historic year for New Brunswick," she said, "and you have indeed a lot to celebrate." And she praised the successive descendants of American Loyalists, Acadians, Irish, Scots and Europeans for accepting the challenges of coexistence.

Ottawa rarely fails her Queen, and the military display greeting her in the national capital was a model of panache and precision. The Queen's contribution to the blaze of colour was her bright scarlet coat, which matched the uniforms around her, the red carpet on which she walked, and the striped awning under which she replied to the Prime Minister's speech of welcome.

Young Sarah Eisen stole the show when she misbehaved prior to the Queen's arrival in *Britannia* (right) at Toronto, then presented her bouquet with the sweetest of smiles (opposite). "We make very

great demands of you," Ontario's Premier told the Queen at the Legislative Building. "It's a very real pleasure," she reassured him (above).

The Six Nations is one of
Canada's largest Indian
reserves, and it was there that
the Queen and Prince Philip
travelled by car after landing in
mid-afternoon at Brantford
Airport. Chief Wellington
Staats was the first to greet
them, acting as host and guide
throughout the thirty-minute

visit. The 10,000 spectators found the Queen relaxed and chatty as she strolled under the pine trees, despite a chilly wind and threatening skies. She dedicated as a National Historic Site the expensively-restored Mohawk Chapel, which provided the backdrop (top) to the ceremony of welcome, and planted her own silver pine in the chapel grounds.

The Six Nations' fierce guardianship of their traditions and culture is just the kind of thing the Queen admires — a

virtue in itself, and a colourful contribution to the Canadian character. She will also have been gratified by the many royal associations boasted by the chapel: the land on which it stands was granted by George III, who also gifted the solid oak coat of arms and the wooden tablets engraved with the Apostles' Creed, Lord's Prayer and Ten Commandments; Queen Anne had sent out a set of Communion silver seventy years earlier; Edward VII granted it royal status in 1904, and one of the stained glass windows now bears the present Queen's cypher. Her visit emphasised the Mohawks' long relationship with the Crown, and Chief Staats asked her specifically "to continue the tradition of watchfulness over the people of the Six Nations."

Prince Philip left the Canadian tour at Sudbury, and the Queen continued the final stage on her own. It took her to Manitoba which, as its Premier was quick to point out, she had last visited all of fourteen years ago. The reminder came at a Provincial Governement dinner, and was reinforced by the Premier's gift of a book of previous royal visits to the province. "I look forward," the Queen responded, "to finding in this volume the threads which my family have contributed to the tapestry of Manitoba's history."

Two of the Queen's more cultural engagements of that day — her last full day in Canada — took her to the Costume Museum at Dugald, for the parade of historical fashions (far left), and to the St Boniface site, in one of Winnipeg's suburbs, where the Voyageurs of the Red River Brigade re-enacted the arrival (left) of La Vérendrye at Fort Maurepas, near Selkirk, 250 years ago. The Queen's guide on her subsequent walk through La Vérendrye Park (opposite) was Mr Justice Michel Monnin (bottom picture), authentically dressed as one of La Vérendrye's sons.

Prime Minister Mulroney greeted the Queen for the last time at the Canadian Government's farewell dinner at the Winnipeg Convention Centre — having himself arrived with his popular wife, Mila, a few minutes earlier. "I am saddened at the task of bidding you farewell," he said. "You and Prince Philip have been models of gracious understanding, sympathetic… and symbolic of our historical evolution." The compliment earned a stalwart response from the Queen: "I shall continue to fulfil my duties as Queen of Canada to the best of my abilities and in the interests of all Canadians."

Undoubtedly the most sensational new line from Diana's 1985 wardrobe is this stunning outfit which she wore at a banquet given by the Mayor of Florence. The low waist is a particularly favourite characteristic, but the rich, black velvet bodice with its sparkling pattern of royal blue stars and spangles had fashion pundits searching for superlatives. Designer Jacques Azagury became a celebrity overnight. Daytime elegance came from Victor Edelstein, with (overleaf) a sophisticated, wine-coloured silk dress finely striped with white. The contrast between the tight, trim cummerbund belt and the fussier bow and sleeves offered a balance well complemented by the wide, matching saucer hat.

Re-cycling has been Diana's fashion hallmark. She had worn this pink ensemble back in 1983, but the Sicilians saw it again, subtly varied, and enhanced by the matching hat with its upturned brim.

Another of Diana's favourites is this striking red suit – a Spanish bullfighter style zoot suit, as it became dubbed in Canada in 1983. Here, Diana wears it for a tour of the Renaissance quarter of Florence, with the subtle addition of a polka-dot blouse underneath. The long lapels and low, straight jacket didn't appeal overmuch to the Italians. "Too much," said one of their fashion experts; "a little provincial." Nevertheless, it was certainly an outfit to catch the eye, and it is doubtful if Diana was too discouraged. Jasper Conran, the suit's designer, would be hard to replace. (Overleaf) the Princess draped in black for her Vatican audience; and more casually dressed for a visit to Milan's churches.

There was a strange irony about Diana's choice of clothes for Thursday, 2nd May, 1985. On what proved to be the sunniest day of the Italian tour with Prince Charles, she was wearing a dress-ensemble overflowing with clouds. The scene was the little port of Trani, one of the prettiest towns in the whole of their 17-day visit, alive with festive decorations and the warmest of welcomes. They

made a leisurely tour of the
11th-century cathedral,
during which fleeting royal
appearances in doorways and
on parapets were greeted with
shouts of "Regina, regina" –
a sure sign that, for the
ebullient and appreciative
Italians at least, Diana was
already their queen. (Over)
the Princess visited the port
of La Spezia after a late
decision to join Prince
Charles who was to have
toured the port alone.

The Italians' send-off was a family affair. Charles and Diana's two young children had joined the Yacht at Venice, and the foursome appeared on her deck – Harry much grown; William slimmer – to wave farewell. These final pictures followed the colourful scenes (overleaf) as the royal couple toured the waterways of Venice.

There was enormous interest in the Prince and Princess of Wales' four-day trip to America late in 1985. Short though it was, it reflected their official lifestyle perfectly: contacts with the Reagans (opposite, bottom left) and the more dependant (bottom); moments of solemnity (left, right) and of recreation (below); and glimpses of Diana in settings formal (far left) and informal (opposite, bottom right).

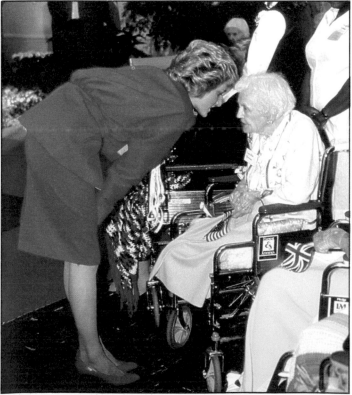

The tour was full of highlights and with never a dull moment. The elation of a polo victory for the Prince (opposite, top left) at Palm Beach contrasted with the poignancy of the terminally ill Jonathan Lollar, whose wish to give Diana a copy of his record (above left) was granted. The chumminess between Princess and First Lady (opposite, top right) proved that the greetings on the night of the White House banquet (far right) were genuinely warm. And the sumptuous display of British goods at J C Penney (right) came second only to that famous gala at Palm Beach's Breakers Hotel (above). As Prince and Princess waved farewell (left) it seemed evident that the future of the monarchy – popular both at home and abroad – was in safe hands.

Prince Andrew became engaged to Sarah Ferguson 19th March 1986. A working girl with a flair for casual clothes (previous pages), Sarah shares Princess Diana's interest in polo and skiing. (Top) her parents' Hampshire home; (left) her own shared house in Clapham.

After weeks of good-natured encounters with the press (above, right) the young couple's affection for each other was at last revealed (left), while Sarah described her ruby and diamond engagement ring (top) as "stunning".